# THE
# NATIVE
# AMERICAN
## EXPERIENCE

〜〜〜 ♀ 〜〜〜

## JAY WERTZ

SEVENOAKS

# Contents

Introduction ¤ 5

In The Beginning—The Ice Age Migration to the Western Hemisphere ¤ 6

The Aboriginal Imprint ¤ 8

Eastern and Woodland Native American Tribes ¤ 10

Conquistadors and the Tribes of the Southwest ¤ 12

The Effects of English and French Colonization ¤ 14

First Contact on the Northwest Coast ¤ 16

Spanish Colonization of New Mexico ¤ 18

Cherokee and Other Tribes and Settlement of the Southeast ¤ 20

Seminoles and the Discovery of Florida ¤ 22

The French and Indian War ¤ 24

The California Mission System ¤ 26

Russian Influence in the Northwest ¤ 28

The New Nation and the Original Inhabitants ¤ 30

Native Americans Encountered by Lewis and Clark ¤ 32

Indian Bureaus and the First Reservations ¤ 34

Gold and Settlers Challenge California Tribes ¤ 36

Native Americans and the Civil War ¤ 38

Farmers, Ranchers, and Native Americans ¤ 40

Last of the Great Warriors—Dakota and Other Plains Tribes ¤ 42

Last of the Great Warriors—Apache and Comanche Tribes ¤ 44

Alaskan and Arctic Tribes Meet the Age of Industrialization ¤ 46

Allotment and Reform—Native Americans Enter the Twentieth Century ¤ 48

The New Deal, Reorganization, and Termination ¤ 50

Fighting on the Other Side—Native American Soldiers ¤ 52

Urban Migration of Native Americans ¤ 54

Outstanding Native Americans ¤ 56

Native American Art and Literature ¤ 58

Moving Forward, Without Forgetting the Past ¤ 60

Index ¤ 62

Credits ¤ 63

# Introduction

**N**ative Americans. The term is the most descriptive of any used to characterize the subjects of this book. Whether they arrived exclusively over the land bridge connecting North America with Asia, a long-held theory, or in combination with a variety of sea-based immigrations, as new research is suggesting, these are truly the original human inhabitants of the continent, and thereby warrant the use of the "native" identifier.

∿∿∿ ☥ ∿∿∿

As one of the most stereotyped groups of people in history, Native Americans have endured a great amount of misunderstanding in the roughly 500 years since continuous contact with Europeans began. Far from being "savages," as they were labeled for centuries, Native Americans had a unique understanding of the land they inhabited and the creatures they shared the world with. Though technology wasn't necessarily at the forefront of their developing cultures, it had a place in them. Their spirituality, however, developed into a complex and extremely important part of their cultures.

The one thing Native Americans did not originally have was a written language, although pictorial communications were used and are discussed in this book. It is therefore, perhaps, unusual to create a history of Native Americans in a work that features documents. But in fact the power of this work is that documents can reveal not just the events, but also the dynamics of a great variety of subjects.

Contact with Europeans, and later, Euro-Americans, has been an integral part of Native American history for the last half millennium. Nothing in the lives of North American Indians has escaped the influence of whites, African Americans, and other later immigrants to the hemisphere. Therefore the treaties, maps, land grants, and declarations that reflect the interactions between Native Americans and other cultures are great aids to understanding the course of history. By the same token, Native Americans had wide-ranging influence on later immigrants to the New World and their enormous impact on the political, economic, and social aspects of North America have continued through the centuries.

Through a combination of textual and visual elements, well-known and rarely seen, an illustrative canvas of many aspects of Native American history and life is offered in this book. It is my fervent hope that this work, influenced by much more expansive legacies, both written and oral, will serve as a conduit to further inspection and study of the rich heritage of the subjects of this book.

*Jay Wertz*
*Los Angeles, California*

# In the Beginning— The Ice Age Migration to the Western Hemisphere

**T**he human preoccupation with "where we came from" is a fascination that can take many forms. These range from simply tracing one's family tree, to advanced genealogy, and all the way to complex interdisciplinary scientific studies which seek to develop theories and establish conclusions about the origins of mankind. And it is no different for the peoples who have inhabited the western hemisphere for thousands of years, the Native Americans, and those who study them. Native American cultures typically hold family and spiritual roots in high regard, and as a consequence the study of their origins commands much attention.

## THE ROLE OF ARCHEOLOGISTS

The study of prehistoric man relies on the work of many scientific disciplines. Without written records, much about Paleo-Indians must be inferred. The role of the archeologist is to discover, retrieve, and interpret physical evidence. The field office of the archeologist is the dig site, a term universally given to the location of objects and remains, whether on the surface, covered by earth and sediment or under water. The home office is the laboratory, where a number of identification techniques are employed. Archeologists combine their findings with the work of geologists, meteorologists, and others to draw conclusions about the objects and remains they discover.

〜〜〜 ⚱ 〜〜〜

The search for Native American origins is a dynamic and continuing process. For centuries, the theories of how man came to inhabit the western hemisphere were varied and sometimes fantastic. One such idea was that early man came from Europe in small boats, following the North Atlantic route later taken by the Vikings. Then, in the early twentieth century, chance discoveries combined with rapidly advancing scientific techniques indicated that humans followed other animals who traveled from northeast Asia, today's Siberia, on to the American continent during the Pleistocene epoch. Around 50,000–80,000 years ago, during the great Ice Age—which actually saw a series of advances and retreats in the polar glaciers—the land mass of Beringia appeared and then disappeared in several cycles. It is often referred to as a bridge between Asia and Alaska. During this time there were several occasions when mankind could have followed large animals across the land bridge, or alternatively moved eastward on watercraft.

The reason archeologists are able to determine the existence of these early humans, now referred to as scientifically as Paleo-Indians, is because evidence such as the discovery of objects made by humans mixed with animal bones substantiates their existence in the New World. Paleontologists, examining fossilized remains of Pleistocene animals such as mammoths, mastodons, sloths, and saber-tooth tigers, made the first recorded discovery of a mixed find in Folsom, New Mexico, in 1926, thereby establishing the first key to dating the Paleo-Indian settlement. More discoveries were made in New Mexico, Colorado, Chile, Mexico, and elsewhere. New scientific techniques, especially Carbon-14 dating, which uses the radioactive decay of naturally occurring isotopes to indicate the age of organic material, confirmed the dates.

From this and other data, a unified theory was developed: that Paleo-Indians crossed Beringia from their previous homes in Siberia in search of big game—the food source that preceded them. They followed the ice-free path down the east face of the Rocky Mountains

**ABOVE LEFT** *The skull of a saber-tooth cat. This carnivore of the Pleistocene Epoch competed for game with man in the late Ice Age.*

**ABOVE** *This biface, or "toolkit," was found in the Lake Manix archeological dig in California's Mojave Desert and is believed to be 14,500 years old. It is called a toolkit because the user would chip off a piece for cutting or scraping, discard the piece, and then repeat the process. When the toolkit was nearly gone, the core was shaped into a spear point.*

**LEFT** *The mastodon and mammoth were different Ice Age species of pachyderm. This skeleton of an adult mastodon was discovered virtually intact in New York State. The artist's rendering of the Wooly Mammoth is based on evidence from paleontological discoveries.*

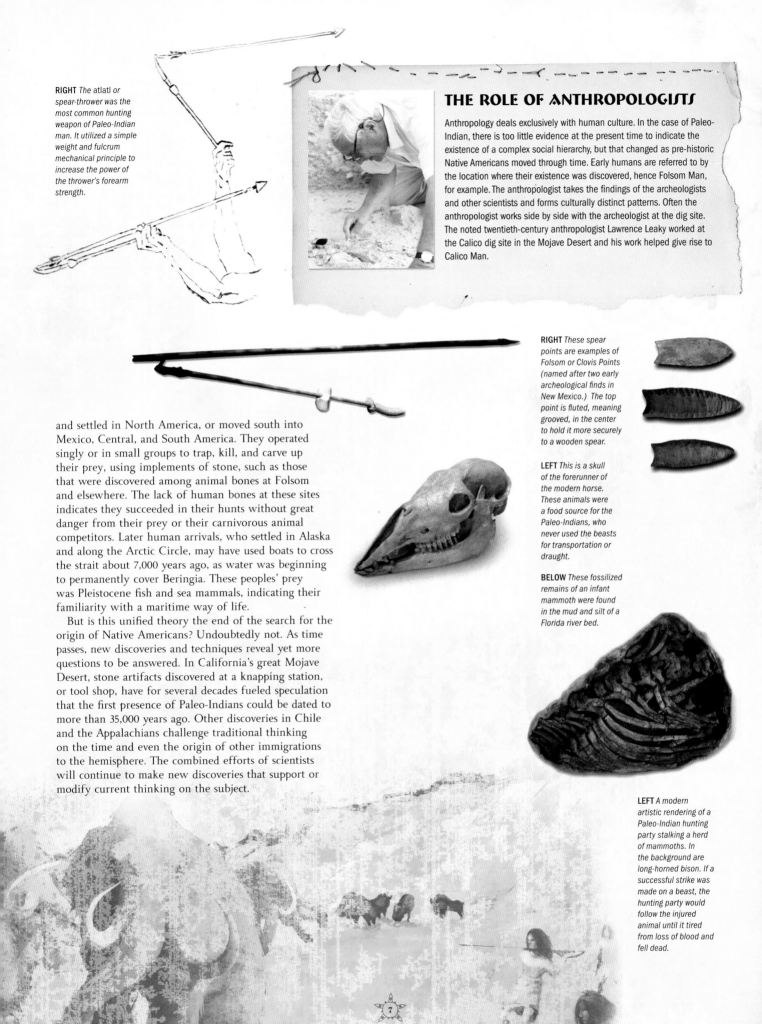

**RIGHT** *The atlatl or spear-thrower was the most common hunting weapon of Paleo-Indian man. It utilized a simple weight and fulcrum mechanical principle to increase the power of the thrower's forearm strength.*

# THE ROLE OF ANTHROPOLOGISTS

Anthropology deals exclusively with human culture. In the case of Paleo-Indian, there is too little evidence at the present time to indicate the existence of a complex social hierarchy, but that changed as pre-historic Native Americans moved through time. Early humans are referred to by the location where their existence was discovered, hence Folsom Man, for example. The anthropologist takes the findings of the archeologists and other scientists and forms culturally distinct patterns. Often the anthropologist works side by side with the archeologist at the dig site. The noted twentieth-century anthropologist Lawrence Leaky worked at the Calico dig site in the Mojave Desert and his work helped give rise to Calico Man.

**RIGHT** *These spear points are examples of Folsom or Clovis Points (named after two early archeological finds in New Mexico.) The top point is fluted, meaning grooved, in the center to hold it more securely to a wooden spear.*

**LEFT** *This is a skull of the forerunner of the modern horse. These animals were a food source for the Paleo-Indians, who never used the beasts for transportation or draught.*

**BELOW** *These fossilized remains of an infant mammoth were found in the mud and silt of a Florida river bed.*

and settled in North America, or moved south into Mexico, Central, and South America. They operated singly or in small groups to trap, kill, and carve up their prey, using implements of stone, such as those that were discovered among animal bones at Folsom and elsewhere. The lack of human bones at these sites indicates they succeeded in their hunts without great danger from their prey or their carnivorous animal competitors. Later human arrivals, who settled in Alaska and along the Arctic Circle, may have used boats to cross the strait about 7,000 years ago, as water was beginning to permanently cover Beringia. These peoples' prey was Pleistocene fish and sea mammals, indicating their familiarity with a maritime way of life.

But is this unified theory the end of the search for the origin of Native Americans? Undoubtedly not. As time passes, new discoveries and techniques reveal yet more questions to be answered. In California's great Mojave Desert, stone artifacts discovered at a knapping station, or tool shop, have for several decades fueled speculation that the first presence of Paleo-Indians could be dated to more than 35,000 years ago. Other discoveries in Chile and the Appalachians challenge traditional thinking on the time and even the origin of other immigrations to the hemisphere. The combined efforts of scientists will continue to make new discoveries that support or modify current thinking on the subject.

**LEFT** *A modern artistic rendering of a Paleo-Indian hunting party stalking a herd of mammoths. In the background are long-horned bison. If a successful strike was made on a beast, the hunting party would follow the injured animal until it tired from loss of blood and fell dead.*

# The Aboriginal Imprint

**Notable Native American Archeological Areas**

**Earliest Period of Findings**
- Paleo-Indian
- Archaic
- Post-Archaic

**T**hree millennia or so before the present time, Paleo-Indian culture was gradually evolving. Just as the search for food had propelled man into the New World, so food became the main driving force behind the formation of groups and cultures (which are today known as tribes.) The large game animals of the Pleistocene epoch were being driven to extinction by ecological factors, such as the drying of the land. Wasteful hunting practices also hastened the extinction, a process which occurred later in the New World—where there were only rougly a million humans spread across two continents—than in the Old World. Although new breeds of animals emerged, the change made man place more attention toward plant food sources.

**ABOVE** *This mask dated to 1700 B.C., is attributed to the Dorset culture, the first Eskimo aboriginal culture, named after Cape Dorset, Alaska, where artifacts from the culture were found. The Dorset Eskimos spread eastward to Newfoundland and the west coast of Greenland, starting in about 3000 B.C.*

The first method of exploiting flora for food was gathering, a relatively simple development, since an abundance of nutritional plant foods existed in most areas. Before long, agriculture, the deliberate cultivation of plants for food, became a part of life in the New World. These Meso-Indians (the successors to the Paleo-Indians) took to agriculture more readily in Mexico and farther south than in the north, probably for ecological reasons. The appearance of advanced city-states among the Inca, Mayan, and Aztecs depended primarily on the rise of agriculture, which freed their populations from the rigors of a transient lifestyle and allowed the establishment of permanent settlements and more complex cultures. The Calusa tribe of Florida, as a large organized community not dependent on agriculture, was a notable exception.

The change also came to Meso-Indians of North

**BACKGROUND**
*Pictograph (painted) and petroglyph (carved) rock art images were a means for early Native Americans to communicate. They could be as simple as an indication of food in the area or range to complex social and spiritual messages.*

**ABOVE RIGHT** *Stone tools of early Native Americans. Shown here are a cutting tool, left, and a spear point from Saskatchewan, Canada.*

America, but more gradually. As reliance on agriculture increased, virtually all the forming cultures of the western hemisphere came to share two distinct traits: a preoccupation with death; and a sense that a higher natural authority controlled the fate of their crops. Care for the dead and worship of—and sometimes sacrifice to—the gods were central features of their cultures, traits which even today Native Americans recognize as an important part of their heritage. Discoveries relating to this phase of development about 3000 B.C. have revealed much about the beliefs and lifestyles of these people. Agricultural tools of the period and new implements of food preparation and storage discovered alongside the points and knives of hunting indicate evolution of lifestyles. More complex cultural themes began to appear. For example, the Adena People and their eventual successors, the Hopewell People, were not only fine artisans of decorative pottery and adornment, they also gave great attention to the dead by building burial mounds. The huge effort in altering the terrain in this way indicated the importance of death and spiritual issues.

## EARLY POTTERY

The shift away from near-exclusive reliance on big game for food led to the development of pottery and baskets, to gather, prepare, cook, and store their foodstuffs. Initially, wild seeds and grains were gathered, and later the three historic staples of the Native American diet: squash, beans, and maize (Indian corn) were grown. Many of these plant foods were prepared by grinding them into meal with the ancient equivalent of a mortar and pestle. Then the meal was liquefied and cooked in a pot or heated immersion style, by dropping hot stones into the vessel.

The term "people" rather than "man" is now used to refer to these societies because the evidence points to cultures and larger groups rather than an individual or single hunting party. Hence the Adena culture relates to discoveries made near that Ohio town. But the names of Native American cultures are also derived from other factors. The Old Copper People, for example, discovered and pounded the naturally occurring metal into shapes. The Red Paint People used a dye made from plants to adorn coffins with the life-inferring color of blood, a symbol of their preoccupation with death.

The Archaic Stage (late hunting/gathering to early agricultural) cultures engaged in trade, as evidenced by their use of raw materials in their artifacts whose natural source was often quite distant. Though few traders ventured long distances, it is likely that cultures traded with those nearby and articles and ideas passed from place to place, one culture at a time. One notable exception was the passage of cultural ideas and items northward from the advanced cultures of Mexico.

**LEFT** *Snow goggles from 500 A.D. The early Eskimos of the Arctic region devised snow goggles like these to prevent snow blindness while traveling across the frozen ground.*

**ABOVE** *This bird effigy ornament from the Hopewell culture was cut from mica by a craftsman. The symmetrical design with one side mirroring the other was common.*

**BELOW** *Stone tools of early Native Americans, top: an adze from the southeastern United States, bottom: a very large obsidian ceremonial blade from Ross County, Ohio.*

However, about 1,800 years ago, a new phase in the evolution of North American cultures began, a period of regression, a kind of "Dark Ages," followed by a period of progressive social change.

By 700 A.D. a new influence spread northward through the Mississippi Valley. From this Mississippian culture, which incorporated pyramids and temples and a hierarchy of priests, the peoples of North America acquired more complex craft and architectural techniques, and a more developed spiritual life. Some scientists see an influence brought from Mexico, while others see the North American mounds, earthen, not stone, as locally developed. Finds in Louisiana dating from 3400 B.C. support the latter theory. The various groups were beginning to divide into tribes, though not necessarily on the basis of language, of which there were half a dozen main tongues and dozens of sub-dialects. All of these developments would continue for several hundred years until the greatest impact on Native American culture in history occurred—first contact with the white man.

**LEFT** *This jar in the shape of a standing human female figure was of the Mississippian culture. The pottery design has a non-symmetrical front and back as a human body does. It was discovered in Cross County, Arkansas.*

**BACKGROUND** *A string of small oval shell beads from the Hopewell culture. Materials were traded among the groups of the Archaic Stage so the Ohio Valley craftsman had mica, obsidian, copper, shell, and other raw elements to use in their creations.*

## MOUND BUILDERS

Beginning with the Adena People (2000 B.C.–200 A.D.) a tradition of burial mounds wove its way into the culture of the North American peoples. Among the Hopewell people, the mounds took on greater size and advanced design. The Mississippian mounds, large, man-made rectangular earthen plateaus topped by temples, are thought to be Mexican influenced. They required a community large enough to provide a workforce of builders, and a social command structure to attain the result. The largest of these mounds discovered is a 16-acre pyramid in the Mississippian city of Cahokia, now in Illinois east of St. Louis. Cahokia, reached the height of its cultural importance around 1000–1100 A.D. Other burial mounds have been discovered in Georgia, Virginia, in Great Lakes glacial kames, and elsewhere.

# Eastern and Woodland Native American Tribes

In the eastern portion of North America, an area bounded roughly on the north by the St. Lawrence River and on the west and south by the lower Ohio and Mississippi rivers, the primordial landscape was covered by dense forests. Here, the prehistoric inhabitants, moving eastward in a search for food and survival, found a different environment to that in the west of the continent. There was large game to be sure, but mastodons and other large game moved less easily through the dense forests and underbrush and were able to disappear more quickly. Here the descendants of the Red Paint People, the Adena-Hopewell, and other ancient groups began to establish a pattern of hunting, fishing, and gathering, and augmented foot travel with an early adaptation of water travel.

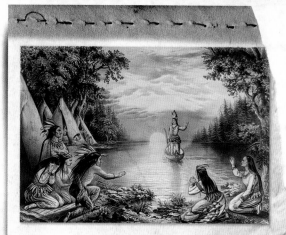

## HIAWATHA

Sometime in the sixteenth century, a Huron prophet named Deganawidah was supposedly inspired through a dream to stop the in-fighting among the Iroquoian speakers. His prophet, Hiawatha—a Mohawk according to the Indian legend that was later fictionalized with some variations by Henry Wadsworth Longfellow—paddled from tribe to tribe, spreading the message of peace and brotherhood. This resulted in the formation of the League of Iroquois Nations. The confederation was formed from the Cayuga, Seneca, Oneida, Mohawk, and Onondaga tribes, with the later inclusion of the Tuscarora. In reality, it may have been the new threat of the white man that caused the tribes to unite.

The first identifiable inhabitants of this region, in what are now eastern Canada and the northeastern and north central United States, were Algonquian speakers. From this common background, tribes developed in dissimilar ways. Some adapted quickly to farming the three staple crops of maize, squash, and beans. Others, in close proximity to the Atlantic Ocean and other bodies of water, derived most of their food from fishing and mollusk gathering. They made use of the abundant forests to gather wood for their fires, to build their homes and construct their watercraft.

Among these tribes were the Micmac, Penobscot, Massachuset, Narraganset, Pequot, Wappinger, Delaware, Nanticoke, and Powhatan. They hunted deer, beaver, rabbit, and game-birds with bow and arrow. Their use of native flint, quartz, and slate produced fine arrowheads and other tools. Many lived in longhouses constructed of elm bark which covered a base of lodge poles made of saplings. The culture had a strong, maternally influenced family base, and many families, with their beds and personal items stacked along the sides, occupied one longhouse. In a center corridor, cooking fires illuminated the interior and produced a great deal of smoke, despite the presence of exhaust cut-outs in the roof. A traditional cross-legged sitting position, which over the years has been attributed to Native Americans, had practical roots. It allowed the longhouse dwellers to conduct their affairs at a level which kept their faces underneath the lingering smoke.

The tribes who lived on the coast substituted smaller conical houses of bark, grouped in small villages, for the longhouses. They gathered clams, lobsters, and mussels from the shoreline and shallow lagoons and fished with nets. Their dugout canoes, adaptable to the interior rivers, were also used to navigate the rocky shorelines of the Atlantic. There was conflict between some tribes; those less adept at farming would raid the corn and squash stocks of their neighbors. A cluster of these Algonquian tribes built up a large empire (known as the Powhatan Confederacy,) which in the sixteenth and seventeenth centuries stretched from the Chesapeake Bay to the coast of present-day North Carolina. All tribes, however, worshipped a higher authority in a nature-based spirit world where gods took the form of animal creatures, the same rabbit, deer, and elk which they hunted.

**ABOVE** *Tee Yee Neen Ho Ga Row was considered an Iroquois emperor and was one of four Mohawk chiefs of Canada on a diplomatic mission to London in 1710. This lithograph is from a painting made during the visit by Jan Verelst.*

**RIGHT** *A wooden dugout canoe, a typical vessel of an eastern tribe. It was discovered submerged on the coast of Connecticut.*

Into this Algonquian world another group of people whose origins are now believed to be in the primal forests of New York, began to expand their influence. These were the Iroquoian speakers who formed the Seneca, Mohawk, Oneida, Cayuga, and Onondaga tribes. They settled the interior of what are now northern Pennsylvania, eastern Ohio, and New York. They also lived in longhouses, traveled in birch-bark canoes, and were skilled hunters with the bow and arrow. A key difference among the Iroquois was the fact that the women owned the dwellings and land and appointed members of the male tribal council, a ruling force with democratic attributes. They sometimes traded and sometimes warred against their neighbors of the Delaware, Susquehanna, and other tribes, and eventually adopted the farming techniques of their neighbors. Another group of Algonquian speakers settled the Great Lakes region, gathering wild rice and eventually turning to farming. These were the Miami, Ottawa, Fox, Ojibwa, and other tribes, and a few Siouan speakers. The Eastern and Woodland tribes settled into a peaceful coexistence, even as a great confederation, the five nations of Iroquois, gave that group immense power in the region. But the balance was interrupted with the coming of European explorers and settlers, beginning in the seventeenth century.

**LEFT** *Black Beaver, born in 1808, was an influential member of the Delaware (Lenape) tribe who traveled throughout North America. The story of the Delaware (the name is completely European in origin) tribe is a sad one. Battled into submission by the Iroquois Confederacy and swindled in land dealings with colonists, they were also one of the tribes hardest hit by European diseases.*

**RIGHT** *Dwellings of the Woodland tribes of the Great Lakes region. Shown here are a conical bison-skin lodge and an oblong birch-bark lodge.*

**BELOW** *This birch-bark bucket of the Penobscot tribe was made from one piece of bark cut to size and sealed with pine tar. The tribes of Maine and eastern Canada made a number of useful containers from bark.*

**Documents**

ITEM 1. Dutchman Willem Janszoon Blaeu, 1571–1638, created this map of the New World in 1635. It is unusual in that the west cardinal point is at the top of the map. New Netherlands, New England and Virginia are identified and some features, such as Long Island, are quite accurately portrayed. Note the illustrations of Indians in canoes in the Atlantic Ocean.

ITEM 2. This 1703 price list of goods sold to Indians uses a measure of beaver pelts, when in season, to compute the cost of European goods and measure the value of other animal skins. For example, two yards of cotton could be had for one beaver pelt. Incredibly, it took eight mink pelts to equal the value of one beaver skin. (See pocket page 19.)

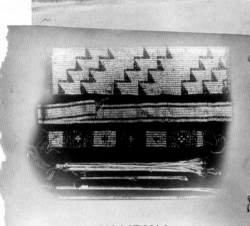

## WAMPUM

Wampum, the Native American form of diplomatic credential and currency, had its origins among the coastal tribes of the east. It gained widespread acceptance among tribes and with European traders as a measure of value and friendship. It was made from small seashells of varying colors that were laboriously ground and shaped to a spherical design, then bored out and strung on tiny cords of sinew. The color, patterns, and designs of the wampum bands had accepted common values. Although much is made of the cheating of Native Americans by the white settlers who traded beads for land, in fact the labor saved in using European glass beads to make wampum strings did give the beads much added value.

**ABOVE** *The wooden ball-headed club was a weapon commonly used by eastern and central Woodland tribes in raids and sometimes open combat and preceded the tomahawk. This Munsee Delaware example was found in southwestern Ontario.*

**LEFT** *The unhappy-looking woman in this lithograph is Sarah Slocum, who was kidnapped and raised by the Lenape sometime in the seventeenth century. European captives were sometimes ransomed back to their people. Others adapted to tribal life.*

# Conquistadors and the Tribes of the Southwest

The early European explorers of western North America arrived from all directions. Besides sea-going explorations of the northwest coast there were incursions down the Mississippi Valley by the French (starting with LaSalle in 1682) and, later, by the British in pursuit of the fur trade. But the first whites to penetrate the southwest were the Spanish conquistadors ("conquerors,") who began to explore the northern part of the continent after Spain established a presence in the New World in the early sixteenth century. These were men of influence who presented their cases before Spanish royalty for the glory of God, their king, and themselves.

Intrigue prevented Hernando de Cortés, the great conquistador of Mexico, from receiving royal approval for his expedition north from Mexico City, the capital of New Spain. Instead, the mission fell to a young and influential soldier-aristocrat, Francisco Vásquez de Coronado, who intended to search for a legendary place of fabulous wealth in gold, the Seven Cities of Cibola, reportedly seen by the off-course survivors of an earlier Spanish expedition from Florida. Coronado followed a trail blazed by a French monk and his guides in 1539 who laid claim to the land for Spain. With a well-equipped group of soldiers and civilians, Coronado set out the following year on a route paralleling the west coast of Mexico, with plans to rendezvous with two ships looking for a northern passage in the Southern Sea (the Pacific Ocean.) The original plan was frustrated when the ships sailed to the head of the Sea of Cortés (Gulf of California) and, unable to proceed, turned back.

Though the land route proved difficult, Coronado's expedition made it to the mythical seven cities, which were actually the Indian pueblos at Zuni, only to find the monk's reports were greatly exaggerated. Further exploration revealed the fertile valley of the Rio Grande

## THE HORSE

The horse, a food source for Paleo-Indian hunters, disappeared from the continent in the Ice Age, but thousands of years later would become the most important non-game animal of Native American life when reintroduced by the Spanish conquistadors. The southwestern tribes were the first to adapt the horse for draft and transportation, stealing or gathering in stray animals from their European conquerors and copying their use. These tribes then started a vigorous trade with their neighbors to the north and gradually the trade worked its way east of the Rockies, and into the hands of the Great Plains tribes with whom the horse has been most closely identified.

**BELOW** White House at Canyon de Chelly National Monument. The structure was built by the Anasazi culture that emerged from the Desert Archaic tradition and was later inhabited by the Navajo who migrated to the Four Corners area. Sitting in the middle of a large Navajo reservation, Cañon de Chelly, as it is known in Spanish, is one of the few places in North America continuously inhabited for more than two millennia.

**BELOW** The west portion of a once expansive three-story pueblo in northwestern New Mexico called Aztec Ruins. Pueblo Indians built the 500-room structure at the height of the early pueblo phase about 1100 A.D. Although the Spanish explored here, the incorrect reference to these Native Americans as Aztecs was made by nineteenth-century Americans who came to the area.

**RIGHT** A wider view of the Canyon de Chelly ruins. As a result of increased raiding when the Civil War began, in 1863–64 U. S. soldiers under militia colonel Kit Carson rounded up more than 8,000 Navajos from their homes in Canyon de Chelly and marched them to the Bosque Redondo Reservation in eastern New Mexico. They were returned to their homes after the war.

**LEFT** Francisco Vásquez de Coronado and his expedition trudge along the Arkansas River in present-day Oklahoma in his final attempt to find "El Dorado," a place of gold. His journey took him as far as Kansas before he turned back.

River in New Mexico, where Coronado and his men were trapped for the winter. Friction with the natives led to the condemnation to death of 200 Indians. The following spring the Pueblo Indians (whose name derives from the Spanish word for a small town,) convinced Coronado to continue his search east and his expedition got as far as Kansas but never found the El Dorado ("gold-laden" place) which they sought. In 1542, Coronado retraced his steps back to Mexico, never to return. It would be 56 years before Don Juan de Oñate led an expedition to New Mexico and established the first permanent settlement there.

The Pueblo tribes encountered by Coronado were descendents of one of three main Indian groups of the semi-arid southwest, the Anasazi. They are discussed in more depth on pages 18–19. The other two groups were the Mogollón and the Hohokam. The Mogollón, who were primarily gatherers, lived in caves or brush dwellings in the high country of the southwest and developed the art of basket-making. Later, they embraced agriculture and began to congregate in villages of small numbers, building round or squared houses of

logs with a base dug three to four feet into the ground. Their culture flourished from around 200 B.C.–1000 A.D. Their descendents are members of the Hopi tribe.

The only early culture of North American Indians to embrace crop farming for their entire food needs also lived in the most arid region of the subcontinent. The Hohokam were wanderers from Mexico who settled in the Gila River valley between 2000 and 200 B.C. What made them so successful was their use of that river's water to irrigate their crops. They spoke two languages, Piman and Yuman. The Piman speakers, by the eighteenth century, had become the Pima and Papagos tribes. They subsisted on crops, wild plants, small game and fish, and were generally friendly to the whites who passed through their villages in large numbers on the trail to California. The Yuman speakers developed into the Yuma, Mohave, Havasupai, and other semi-nomadic tribes that settled the Colorado River area of what is now Arizona and California. The most successful planters, such as the Havasupai, established trade with their less agriculturally successful neighbors.

To the east of the Hohokam descendents were a group of more recent Athapaskan-speaking arrivals to the New World, the Apaches. They were nomads, like the tribes of the southern plains with whom they would intermix, the Comanches and the Kiowa. Raiders, they preyed on neighboring tribes and, eventually, on the white man. Another Athapaskan-speaking tribe, the Navajo, settled the mountainous area where New Mexico's boundary now joins three other states. They combined aggressive raiding on their Pueblo neighbors with successful agriculture. Their location in this isolated section of the southwest, and their environment, would eventually lead them to become the largest tribe in North America.

## IRRIGATION

The basis of modern agriculture in the southwest United States is irrigation. This was developed by the Hohokam and adopted by their descendents. The Hohokam tapped the Gila River and its tributaries to bring water to their maize fields. Their engineering technique was deceptively simple; they let the water flow into the canals as they dug, using the depth of water they stood in to judge whether each channel was too shallow or too deep. Later, the Pimas used the irrigation canals to expand their crop line from maize to include squash and kidney beans, and to achieve great yields of wheat.

# The Effects of English and French Colonization

**T**he idyllic image of a Thanksgiving feast, in which Native Americans and white settlers celebrated a successful harvest season, belies the often bloody and mostly deadly effects of French and English colonization on the natives of North America. The feast probably did take place, a result of the sheltering of the Plymouth Colony by Chief Massasoit of the Wampanoag tribe in 1621, who was seeking allies against his enemy, the Narraganset.

From the early exploration by England's John Cabot at the end of the fifteenth century, North America became a prize to be competed over by England, France and, to a lesser extent, other European countries. Even before colonization began, European explorers and fishermen who dropped anchor along the Atlantic Coast and entered its inlets became a source of curiosity and disease for the American natives. The problem of disease was aggravated as France and England, seeing the riches of gold, silver, and other valuables brought from the New World by the Spanish galleons they captured, created chartered companies to colonize North America.

England first claimed a colony in Newfoundland in 1583 to aid its fishing interests there. The Virginia Company, led by Sir Walter Raleigh, was granted a charter by Queen Elizabeth I with the provision of being able to take any land inhabited by non-Christians. The colony, was established on Roanoke Island, now part of North Carolina, in 1585, lasted only three years, its survivors captured or melded into the local native population.

> *"Where the English come to settle, a Divine Hand makes way for them, by removing or cutting off the Indians, either by Wars one with the other, or by some raging mortal Disease"*
> **Daniel Denton, 1670**

**ABOVE** *Pocahontas interceding for the life of Captain John Smith in 1608. Although the English ungratefully kidnapped her four years later to ransom peace with her father Powhatan, Pocahontas became the first widely known Native American celebrity in Europe.*

## POCAHONTAS

Pocahontas was born Matowaka, but her father, the powerful chief Powhatan, referred to her as Pakahantes meaning "my favorite daughter." Captain John Smith claimed that the teenage girl put herself between him and the executioner's axe when Smith was a Powhatan captive. Whether or not this is true, she became the most famous Native American female among Europeans in the seventeenth century. In 1612 she was held hostage by the English and fell in love with and married the colonist John Rolfe. Powhatan kept peace with the colonists until his death in 1618. Pocahontas became a Christian, sailed to England and was presented to the Court of King Charles I, but died of smallpox in 1617 before returning to the colonies. Her son, Thomas Rolfe, was one of the most powerful leaders of colonial Virginia.

# BOW AND ARROW

In the early days of the Jamestown Settlement, an Englishman challenged a friendly native to shoot an arrow through a leather-covered wood shield about three feet in diameter. To the astonishment of the European, the arrow dug a foot deep into the target. Sometime in the Archaic period, Native Americans discovered that animal sinew could be stretched and dried, attached to a flexible piece of wood and used to propel a stone-tipped stick through the air. European metal made arrow tips more deadly. Even after the introduction of firearms, many warriors preferred the time-tested bow and arrow for horseback hunting and warfare.

**RIGHT** *Four examples of chipped stone arrowheads. Arrowheads were produced by nearly every North American Indian tribe from the Archaic Stage forward, including the Algonquian and Iroquoian speakers of the eastern and central Woodlands.*

The next attempt by the Virginia Company would be at Jamestown in 1607. The difficult conditions nearly led the colony to founder. Among their troubles were attacks by warriors from the Pamunkey and other members of the 200-village Powhatan Confederacy. The colony survived in part when the confederation's leader, Powhatan, made peace with the Virginia Company after his daughter, Pocahontas, married an Englishman in 1612. Trade began and tobacco was discovered, a cash crop that would ultimately lead to a prosperous Virginia. After Powhatan's death in 1618, a wave of violence spread, breaking out in 1622 and again 22 years later. By that time, however, the colonists greatly outnumbered the Indians and the Native American fate in the region was effectively sealed.

In the seventeenth century the French began to found colonies in what is now Nova Scotia and at the mouth of the St. Lawrence River. New France took on permanence when Samuel de Champlain established Québec in 1608. At that time, the powerful Huron tribe controlled the area. The French brought Catholic missionaries with them, but it would be many years before they obtained any converts to the Catholic religion. As French influence spread over eastern Canada, fur trading quickly became a viable industry. The Iroquois Confederacy was being wooed by the Dutch, who were establishing their own colonial settlements in the Hudson River valley. Competition between the English of the rapidly expanding colonies of New England and the Dutch caused the Iroquois to wage war on neighboring tribes as the demands of the fur trade outran the supply the Confederacy could muster on their own lands. They attacked the tribes to the south, including the Delaware, and to the north, challenging the Huron along the St. Lawrence and conquering the Erie in 1654. Meanwhile, French traders established posts in the Great Lakes region to extend their trade and power. Raids and devastating wars broke out in other areas of the colonies as the European powers used intertribal warfare to consolidate their own gains in power and land, as occurred during the War of the Spanish Succession (1701–14.)

**TOP** *William Penn's treaty with the Indians under the elm tree at Shackamaxon, in what is now Pennsylvania, represented the Quaker leader's honest attempt to make peace with the tribes in his proprietorship. However, his son would undermine his father's fair dealings with Indians when he came to power.*

**BACKGROUND** *An illustrative map of New Sweden published in a Thomas Campanius Holms book in 1702. The Swedish settled among the Susquehannock and Lenape tribes on Delaware Bay by establishing a settlement called Christiana. By 1655, however, New Sweden was absorbed by the more powerful Dutch in the area and finally the area became the Delaware Colony of William Penn's proprietorship.*

**LEFT** *Henry Hudson, who discovered the river bearing his name and the rich fur country of upstate New York in 1609, offers liquor to the Indians on the North River (now the Hudson.) Alcohol was a dangerous substance, particularly in the hands of those unaccustomed to its use, and colonial governments sought to ban its sale to Native Americans. But opportunists saw it as a tool of manipulation.*

# First Contact on the Northwest Coast

A long, narrow ribbon of land stretches from the peninsular region of Alaska to just beyond the southern border of today's Oregon. Faced on the east by the Cascade Range and the northern reaches of the Rocky Mountains, and on the west by the Pacific Ocean, it is a region of natural beauty and rich resources. Into this region came the first people of the future Native American tribes of the northwest. They were probably some of the last to cross the land bridge, and the record of their history goes back 4,000 years. They are people concerned in the utmost with their past, and their ancestral heritage dominates major aspects of their lives.

Hemmed in by the mountains and living on an even narrower strip of rocky coast with only occasional narrow beaches were the Tlingit, Haida, Tsimshian, Kwakiutl, Nootka, Makah, Salish, Quinault, Chinook, and other tribes. They came from three major linguistic stocks: Athapaskan, like their neighbors to the north and east, and two of the more obscure forms of Algonquian. Culturally they shared many traits, however, with lineage and class society being among the most prominent. Another shared trait, almost unheard of in other Native American cultures, was a complete lack of agriculture. With 100 inches (250 cm) of annual rainfall and a mild and moist climate determined by the mountain barrier and warm Japanese Current offshore, there was no need for it. Fauna was abundant in the dense evergreen forests, and aquatic food sources were even more readily available.

Besides hunting, fishing, and the occasional gathering of wild plants for food, another environmental factor defined the culture. The forests of pine, spruce, and especially red and yellow cedar made these tribes woodcrafters of superlative ability. Their skill was not only utilitarian, for the construction of dwellings and water-craft, but also possessed an aesthetic sense for sophisticated carving and crafting techniques. With simple non-metallic tools, these woodworkers cut and carved houses up to 60 feet (18 m) in length, canoes which ranged in size up to the same upper limit, fashioned from a single downed tree, and hundreds of other useful and decorative items. They traveled by canoe on the rivers and open sea in search of food and as war parties, which were usually assembled for acquiring slaves, or occasionally for retribution of some wrong caused by an affront to a village chief.

**ABOVE** *A shell necklace of Nuu-chah-nulth origin from 1780.*

**LEFT** *Tlingit men go to sea in an ocean-going canoe at Lituya Bay, Alaska in this French engraving from 1786.*

**BACKGROUND** *In this 1786 engraving Nootka canoes approach a European sailing ship in Cook's Harbor, Alaska. Early curiosity about the strange-looking sea-craft soon led to active trade between the aboriginal people of the Northwest and the ships that anchored in the protected waters near their homes.*

**BELOW LEFT** *Fort Vancouver, on the Columbia River, near its confluence with the Willamette River, in present-day Washington, began as a trading post and regional headquarters for the Hudson's Bay Company. Pictured in this woodcut is its later incarnation as a U.S. Army outpost.*

## TOTEM POLES

The totem pole as a free-standing carved wooden representation of northwest Indian culture is a fairly recent phenomenon, appearing around the early nineteenth century. Originally the carved cedar logs were produced as center posts and entrances to the large wooden houses in which kinfolk and clans coexisted. The animal figures represented the family crest of the house and occasionally tributes to the deeds of departed relatives. Whites became fascinated with them and the poles were adapted as free-standing signposts to villages and the clans and kinfolk that inhabited and, therefore, controlled stretches of the coastline. Although originally denounced by church and government as pagan symbols, the twentieth century saw a rebirth of the totem pole as a cultural symbol.

One of the most fascinating and contradictory aspects of the northwest coast Native American culture was the Potlatch, from the Nootka word "give." The Potlatch was a great feast in which a family chief and his clan expended a stockpile of goods that had been accumulated for months (sometimes years) to stage a large feast, often as part of a wedding or coming-of-age ceremony, for invited guests from another clan or village. The result of the potlatch sometimes sunk a chief into a period of indigence. For a culture in which chiefs measured status by the accumulation of wealth, this seems incongruous behavior. Yet there was a catch. The guest chief and his clan would be expected to repay their host, with interest, in the form of an even larger feast with more gifts at some time in the future.

**ABOVE** *A camp of Chinook Indians at The Dalles, Oregon on the Columbia River. Fish dry on one of the tent poles. Mount Hood is pictured in the background.*

**LEFT** *A Quinault girl wears ornaments made of shells meticulously strung together in this Edward Curtis photograph.*

First contact came with the explorers who arrived in the small inlets around the upper peninsula of Washington and Vancouver Island in 1775. A lively trade developed and, while there was some individual strife over cheating on both sides, the bartering flourished and soon the metal objects, cloth, and bright colored bangles brought by the European ships were redistributed to tribes in exchange for pelts, woodcarvings, and pearls. One tribe on the southern edge of the culture, the Chinooks, already had a reputation as a trading band, and the new goods they acquired enhanced this, since they traded not only along the northwest coast, but also with the tribes of northern California and the plateau region. The tribes of the northwest coast never engaged in full-scale war with the whites, although several groups of skirmishes occuring in the nineteenth century, such as Kamiakin's War, reached larger proportions as missionaries, settlers, and government intrusion began to affect their long-established ways of life.

**BELOW LEFT** *This nineteenth-century lithograph shows a group of Skagit men preparing to launch their canoes from Whidbey Island, in what is now Washington state. Mount Rainier appears in the background.*

**BELOW** *This wooden double chest is of Tsimshian origin, a tribe from northern British Columbia. It is carved on four sides to represent a mythical sea monster.*

**ABOVE** *This interior of a Coast Salish dwelling was painted by Paul Kane, one of the talented nineteenth-century painters who portrayed Native American life. He spent time among the Coast Salish in 1847. Here, one woman spins while another weaves a blanket. The raw materials for these textiles were wool from the mountain goat and hair from a specially bred dog (pictured.) That breed is now extinct.*

# Spanish Colonization of New Mexico

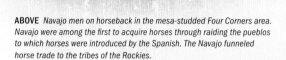

Of all the tribes of the arid southwest, the Anasazi (Navajo for "old ones") were the most architecturally prolific. But the familiar adobe pueblo was not the initial dwelling of these people of the Desert Tradition that were influenced by Hohokam and Mollogón traditions but were distinct in other ways. Geographically they inhabited the Four Corners area where present-day Colorado, New Mexico, Utah, and Arizona join. Chronologically, the culture began about 1 A.D. and at the time the dwellings were rounded mud huts, partially subterranean. Their culture prospered on good maize growing with ample summer rains. Gradually they underwent a change that caused them to abandon their semi-subterranean houses for square houses of dried adobe or adobe bricks. By 750 A.D. these homes were joined by common walls and even stacked as kin and clans lived in adjoining units in the desert canyons.

**ABOVE** *Navajo men on horseback in the mesa-studded Four Corners area. Navajo were among the first to acquire horses through raiding the pueblos to which horses were introduced by the Spanish. The Navajo funneled horse trade to the tribes of the Rockies.*

**ABOVE** *The Anasazi cliff dwellings at Mesa Verde National Park, Colorado. The multi-structure cities were built high in mesa cliffs for protection from hostile tribes. Circular religious houses have a deep hole in the floor, "sipapu," to symbolize the rise from the earth of ancestors. Mesa Verde and nearby Canyon of the Ancients National Monument contain a large number of dwellings and rock paintings of the Anasazi.*

**RIGHT** *Hopi dwellings at Walpi. On a group of mesas in northeastern Arizona sit the eight pueblo communities who speak Hopi and one pueblo of refugees from Spanish occupation of the Rio Grande valley.*

By 1050 A.D. the pueblos had evolved into large villages. Pueblo Bonita in Chaco Canyon, for example, had 800 units. But the competition among pueblos led to the abandonment of the canyon homes and the Anasazi migrated to the cliffs of the mesas, building the same compartmentalized dwelling villages on top of high plateaus, or in protected areas of the mesa cliffs. The climate was changing and about three hundred years later these dwellings were also abandoned. Most clans settled in the fertile Rio Grande valley of northern New Mexico and areas of west Texas. The Anasazi as a culture gave way to the pueblo tribes in these areas, including the Hopi, who established villages in northeast Arizona, and the Zuni, who established a large community midway between the Hopi and the Rio Grande valley settlers.

It was the Zuni pueblo that was the subject of stories told by survivors of a disastrous Spanish mission to Florida who traveled overland to the west and finally to Mexico. Called the Seven Cities of Cibola, it was the first southwestern community visited by Francisco Vásquez de Coronado in 1540.

**RIGHT** *A Navajo first-phase chief-style blanket (early 1800s) of handspun churro wool. An archeological discovery dates this technique in patterns of horizontal stripes of white, brown, and indigo to 1750 or earlier. Navajo blankets were in great demand as social expressions, and in trade. Plains Indians would trade as many as ten bison robes for a quality blanket.*

## PUEBLO DRESS

The modern Pueblo Native American wears a combination of traditional and western-style clothing. The men wear a cotton shirt over a pair of cotton trousers that end just below the knees. A sash, usually yellow, or leather belt with silver adornment is worn round the waist. The more traditional breech cloth or G-string is only used for ceremonial purposes, along with a feather headdress. The women wear a rectangular woolen garment in black or brown called a *manta* which is tied over the right shoulder and under the left arm. It is often decorated at the hem with red or blue trim. A hemmed skirt is worn underneath, tied with a sash at the waist, and from the Spanish influence a slip is worn underneath and an apron in front, and perhaps a shawl. Both sexes use blanket wraps for cold weather and wear hard moccasins, the women preferring white moccasins or boots. Hopi maidens often wear their hair in the symbolic butterfly style shown here.

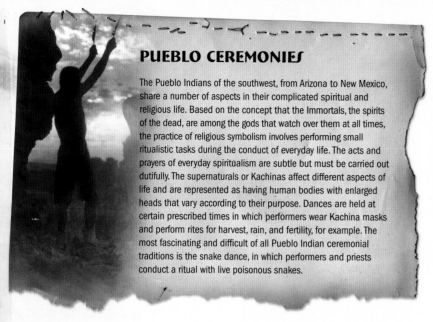

# PUEBLO CEREMONIES

The Pueblo Indians of the southwest, from Arizona to New Mexico, share a number of aspects in their complicated spiritual and religious life. Based on the concept that the Immortals, the spirits of the dead, are among the gods that watch over them at all times, the practice of religious symbolism involves performing small ritualistic tasks during the conduct of everyday life. The acts and prayers of everyday spiritualism are subtle but must be carried out dutifully. The supernaturals or Kachinas affect different aspects of life and are represented as having human bodies with enlarged heads that vary according to their purpose. Dances are held at certain prescribed times in which performers wear Kachina masks and perform rites for harvest, rain, and fertility, for example. The most fascinating and difficult of all Pueblo Indian ceremonial traditions is the snake dance, in which performers and priests conduct a ritual with live poisonous snakes.

**ABOVE** A Navajo hogan in Window Rock, Arizona. The hogan was traditionally earthen and built over three large poles covered by brush with two smaller poles making an eastward-facing doorway. The floor was dug about a foot (30 cm) deep to provide an interior bench along the walls. This improvement on the old style features some horizontal log substructure, but is still earth-covered.

Finding the reports of those who preceded him greatly exaggerated, Coronado moved east and spent the winter among the pueblos in the Rio Grande valley. The Pueblo Indians sent Coronado east in his search for gold and were rid of the Spanish for 60 years.

Then an expedition of Spanish and Mexican Indians arrived under the command of Juan de Oñate to colonize the Rio Grande Valley. At first the pueblo dwellers were satisfied with a peaceful coexistence side by side with the newcomers and even allowed the building of Catholic churches among the pueblos. The traditional place for the Indians to meditate, socialize and conduct spiritual ceremonies was the kiva, a rounded and domed adobe room reminiscent of the original Anasazi dwellings. An open hole in the roof represented the ascendancy of man into the Upper World. But the Spanish friars insisted the Indians abandon their traditional beliefs and submit to their strict form of Christianity with harsh punishment for those who didn't.

At dawn on August 10, 1680 the Pueblo Indians and some of the mixed-blood immigrants revolted against the oppression of the missionaries, slaughtering about 400 Spaniards. The survivors fled to Sante Fe, then El Paso. Another expedition arrived 12 years later and offered coexistence of the two cultures. The pueblo people compromised as well, accepting some principles of Christianity while practicing their traditional religion. For the remaining few years of the sixteenth century and the next two centuries, the Pueblo Indians were mostly unaffected by the changing political landscape of the region, and they remain the most settled in their ancestral lands and culture of all North American Indians.

**LEFT** A contemporary artistic rendering of the Wupatki pueblo near Flagstaff, Arizona. The twelfth-century pueblo was a late starter in an extremely arid area. But it is thought that spring water in the area, which is also served by the Little Colorado River, encouraged the building of the complex in a region where evidence indicates Native American presence from 11,000 B.C.

**LEFT** The terraced homes of the Zuni pueblo. Zuni are descendants of the Mogollon. A single pueblo remains near the western border of the state of New Mexico, where once there were many, including the Hawikuh Pueblo, the influence for the legend of the Seven Cites of Cibola.

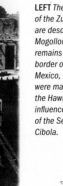

**BELOW LEFT** A Kachina doll in the form of a group of koshares (sacred clowns) participating in a pueblo ceremony. The koshares were painted from head to foot in black and white stripes with their hair tied with corn husks. They channeled the spirit of fertility in dances and provided comic relief during ceremonies.

**BELOW RIGHT** The Hopi pueblo of Old Oraibi. The western pueblos were built of stone and faced with adobe while eastern pueblos were made of unbaked adobe bricks. Ladder entrances through the roof, for protection from enemies, have largely given way to ground-floor screen doors.

# Cherokee and Other Tribes and Settlement of the Southeast

The Appalachian foothills of the southeast were home to the dynamic tribe of Iroquoian speakers known since first contact as the Cherokees. Their lands comprised what are now parts of western Virginia, eastern Kentucky and Tennessee, and northern Georgia and Alabama. Like their distant Iroquois relatives to the north, they were a maternally-based culture, with clans forming around the women, who also selected leadership positions in the mostly democratic tribal council. The females owned the lands and thatched-roof dwellings that were scattered among many small clan-based villages. They were successful farmers, fishermen in the fresh water streams running down from the mountains, and hunters of all kinds of game.

**ABOVE** *Elias Boudinot (Buck Watie) was a highly educated member of an influential Cherokee family. He assumed his new name from a member of the Continental Congress who took an interest in him. Boudinot was the first editor of the Cherokee Phoenix and worked tirelessly for the education of his people. One of the Cherokees who were resigned early on to the forced move to Indian Territory, he was executed there on June 22, 1839 by a faction of Cherokees who viewed his acceptance of the government movement order as treason.*

MMMM ⚱ MMMM

The Cherokees' neighbors to the east were the Algonquian-speaking Catawba, while to the west and south were the Muskogean speakers, the Choctaws, Chickasaws, and Creeks. The latter was a name given by the colonists because the Creek villages were usually found on river banks. They had a semi-socialistic culture in which a supreme ruler, a *mico*, was appointed for life, but had no absolute power. He was advised by a group of senior tribesmen in community affairs. Like the Cherokees, the Creeks had a maternal predominance. Intermarriage was strictly taboo, and clans were identified with animal names. The socialistic aspect of their culture was the practice of communal,

## HARVEST FESTIVALS

Because of favorable climatic conditions, the agricultural output of southeastern tribes was usually abundant. The great importance they placed on the gods for their agricultural success is manifested in their celebration of harvest festivals. At the four-day green corn festival or "busk" celebrated by the Creeks, all old clothing and household goods were burned and replaced by new items. All criminal offenders except for murderers were pardoned and the community feasted on deer and the new crop of maize. Games were played, including the original form of lacrosse, and dances were held. Men underwent ritual cleansing by imbibing an herbal drink.

**ABOVE** *This barbed spear point was painstakingly chipped from natural stone by a member of a southeastern tribe. The barbs took hold better when the spear point penetrated the flesh of game.*

**LEFT** *At the end of the Civil War, emancipated slaves formerly owned by Cherokees, such as this mother and child sitting in front of their cabin in Fort Gibson, Indian Territory, became eligible for citizenship in the Cherokee Nation.*

as well as individual, agriculture for visitors and the indigent. Some Creek villages were peaceful and others warlike. The Choctaw and Chickasaw cultures were in many respects similar to that of the Creek. These two tribes resided principally in what are now Mississippi and southern Alabama.

When trouble began with the neighboring Catawba and Creek tribes, the Cherokees formed larger villages and pacts between them to fight their enemies. Contact with Europeans heightened the friction between the groups. As French and British trappers and traders entered the region in the eighteenth century, the Cherokee aligned themselves with one or the other. The Creeks favored the British, but a group split off from the tribe and eventually became the Seminoles. European trade goods empowered tribal leaders, and a great deal of intermarriage began between the English and Scottish men who came into the region and Creek and Cherokee women. The offspring of these unions were readily accepted into the tribe. Well armed with British muskets by the time of the American Revolution, the Cherokee, incensed by the influx of settlers, fought for the British against the colonists and their allies, the Catawba. The Creeks, Choctaw, and Chickasaws tried to stay out of the wars between white men.

By the end of the War of Independence, the strongest community of Cherokees was situated in northwest Georgia, centering around a settlement on the Etowah River. Even though they maintained their tribal independence, the Cherokee assimilated European culture, language, clothing, and education to a great degree. Some expanded their agricultural holdings into plantation size, grew and traded cash crops, and even owned slaves. Eventually they signed treaties with the new American government and fought alongside Andrew Jackson in the hope of maintaining their ancestral lands. But that hope would be dashed despite their ambitious political and diplomatic efforts to influence their own destiny.

**Document**
ITEM 5. The *Cherokee Phoenix* newspaper began in 1828 with parallel columns in English and the Cherokee language devised by the Sequoyah. It was a significant attribute of the Cherokee culture when it was at its apex in Georgie, and dealt with issues important to the Cherokees, including their freedom.
(See pocket page 31.)

**BELOW** *Joseph Vann was a wealthy mixed-blood Cherokee who lost his life and those of 52 others during a river race in 1844.*

**RIGHT** *This 1885 illustration by John White of Pomeioc village in North Carolina shows a typical southeastern village, with bark lodges built in a circular pattern around a common area.*

The Secretaries of the several Temperance Societies in the Nation, are respectfully requested, to forward, immediately, to the undersigned, a list of the names of all persons who have united with their respective Societies during the past year; and also any other information that may be valuable, or interesting, connected with the progress of Temperance among the Cherokees, within the same time.
WILL. P. ROSS,
Sec. Cher. Tem. Society.
Sept. 25, 1845.

**BACKGROUND** *The Cherokee nation was split on slavery. Many Cherokees brought their slaves with them to Indian Territory, traded slaves, and offered rewards for the capture of runaways, as this 1845 announcement in the Cherokee Advocate attests. But other Cherokees harbored the fugitives until the Confederate defeat in the Civil War sealed their emancipation.*

### SEQUOYAH

Sequoyah, also known as George Geist, was a Cherokee of mixed blood, with a German trader father and Native American mother. He was raised in the Cherokee culture and supposedly never learned English. After a crippling accident, he devised an alphabet of the Cherokee language that was made up of about 80 characters. It was enthusiastically accepted and widely studied. Many Cherokees became literate, and in 1828 the first Native American weekly newspaper was printed. The inaugural issue included Sequoyah's thoughts promoting the Cherokee ideal of independent sovereignty.

**RIGHT** *This pipe carved in the shape of a duck was found in Georgia's Clay County, an area where there are also burial mounds. It is made from steatite, a popular stone used in early carvings.*

# Seminoles and the Discovery of Florida

**BELOW LEFT** *Billy Bowlegs, the Seminole warrior known as the "Alligator Chief." Bowlegs fought in the Second Seminole War and was among a group that took refuge in the Everglades. They were left alone for a few years until trouble began as white settlement greatly increased in south Florida. He led Seminoles resisting removal against the U.S. government in 1857 but was captured and removed to Indian Territory in 1858. Bowlegs was a skilled diplomat and spoke three languages—and was not, in fact, bowlegged.*

Even though they are popularly seen as the tribe most associated with Florida, the Seminoles (Sim-a-no'le, meaning "runaways") were actually an offshoot of the Muskogean-speaking Creeks who "discovered" Florida in the early eighteenth century. Long before them, other tribes—the Guale, Apalachee, Timucua, Tekesta, and Calusa—inhabited the Florida panhandle and peninsula. Other than water-borne trading with tribes from nearby Caribbean islands, these Native Americans had very little contact with the outside world. That changed after Christopher Columbus's discovery in 1492 of Hispaniola in the Caribbean while searching for a western passage to the Far East; his belief that he had reached the East Indies led to the coining of the misnomer "Indians" for Native Americans. Columbus's discoveries resulted in Spanish exploration of the land to the north. Florida was twice explored by Ponce de León (in 1513 and 1521) and invaded by Spanish landing parties on both coasts.

Yet the Native American tribes of Florida avoided the fate of their fellow natives in Central and South America until the 1560s, when France sent several ships to northern Florida and Fort Caroline was established on what is now St. John's River.

## DISEASES

Deadly as the muskets and cannon of the Europeans were to Native Americans during the first several centuries of contact, new diseases were more fatal to the populations of many tribes. Serious diseases such as smallpox, yellow fever, and bubonic plague were unknown in the western hemisphere prior to first contact. Less serious diseases in Europe such as measles, mumps, and whooping cough were often fatal to the Native Americans, who had no immunity to them. A mysterious epidemic spread through New England in 1616–18, killing more than 150,000 Native Americans, including 90 percent of the Wampanoag tribe. The number of Native Americans who died from diseases can only be estimated but it was a major reason for the decline of the population to an all-time low by 1850.

- **PRE-CONTACT DISEASES**
  *Tuberculosis, Venereal Syphilis*
- **DISEASES FROM EUROPE**
  *Smallpox, Measles, Cholera, Bubonic Plague, Typhoid, Scarlet Fever, Pleurisy, Diphtheria, Mumps, Whooping Cough, Gonorrhea, Chancroid, Typhus*
- **DISEASES FROM AFRICA**
  *Malaria, Yellow Fever, Dysentery*
- **INTRODUCED SOCIAL DISEASE**
  *Alcoholism*

The Spanish returned in 1565 to found St. Augustine as the first permanent and lasting settlement in Florida. They wiped out their French rivals by destroying Fort Caroline and its relief expedition. The Spanish then sent explorers and Christian missionaries to establish peace and trade with the natives from present-day South Carolina to Pensacola. The inland Creeks, surrounded by enemies, sought Spanish arms and invited Spanish missionaries to their villages in 1681. Within a few years, they had found a better ally in English-speaking traders from South Carolina. These well-armed Creeks then attacked Spanish missions in northern Florida, as well as their Indian enemies to the west. Just after the turn of the eighteenth century, England entered one of the series of wars between European powers, the War of Spanish Succession. In 1702, the English royal governor of South Carolina, James Moore, attempted unsuccessfully to take St. Augustine from the Spanish by force. But his expedition was turned back after a fleet of Spanish ships overtook them. Moore

**LEFT** *Nea-Math-La was a Seminole chief during the Second Seminole War. In 1836 he was captured by Alabama militiamen and sent in chains to Indian Territory.*

**BELOW LEFT** *A lithograph of Hernando de Soto and his landing party at Tampa Bay 1539. De Soto not only brought soldiers, but also priests, artisans, tools, and livestock to begin his gold-seeking expedition from an established city, which he called Espiritu Santo, present-day Bradenton. From there he launched a three-year campaign in search of El Dorado, terrorizing, killing, and enslaving Indians along the way, finding no gold, only death, on the banks of the Mississippi River.*

then dispatched Creek war parties to raid St. Augustine and Spanish strongholds. The Creek war parties raided villages of the Florida tribes too and the violence went on in Florida for years. Disease also affected the native Florida tribes and the Seminole invaders. It would be decades before the Seminoles established a strong presence in the area.

By the early 1800s, the Seminoles found themselves facing a new enemy. Andrew Jackson, the hero of the stunning victory against the British at New Orleans in 1815, had been achieving significant military success against the Indians. After defeating the Red Sticks (northern Creeks) at the Battle of Horseshoe Bend in March 1814 with the aid of southern Creeks and Cherokees, he signed a treaty that gained 20 million acres of Native American land for the United States. In December 1817, President James Madison ordered Jackson to wage war against Creeks and Seminoles in Georgia, under the pretext of preventing runaway slaves from escaping to Florida to join the Seminoles. The campaign was a tacit attempt to gain Florida from the Spanish. Jackson and his Tennessee volunteers were attacked by Seminole warriors near Pensacola, but Jackson eluded the warriors and sacked and destroyed their villages. He then attacked Pensacola, deposed the Spanish governor, and found evidence that Spanish and British subjects there were supplying weapons to the Indians. The First Seminole War ended in 1818 and Spain ceded Florida to the United States in 1819, with Jackson becoming its territorial governor. The Seminoles would continue to fight for decades to maintain their homes in Florida, but most were finally removed, except for a small group that disappeared into the Florida everglades.

**LEFT** *A colorfully dressed Seminole man hunts gar fish in the backwaters of Florida from a sturdy canoe. An able fisherman can snare a fish with a lightning-quick thrust of the spear.*

**BELOW LEFT**
*A Seminole woman poses in a European-style dress and shawl with her baby secured to her back. Because of the Seminole policy to welcome runaway slaves from both the Southern states and the Caribbean, and adopt them into their villages, a number of those in the Native American and African cultures intermarried.*

**BELOW RIGHT** *This deep buff ware bowl with an unusual flanged rim was discovered at Crystal River in Citrus County, Florida. The area on Florida's west coast has been set aside as a protected archeological park.*

**BACKGROUND**
*A drawing of Fort Caroline on Florida's St. John's River as seen from above. Fort Caroline was an attempt to establish a foothold in an area of Spanish domination. In 1564 Rene de Laudonniere built the fort with 200 French colonists. A year later the Spanish king sent Pedro Menéndez de Avilés to attack the reinforced fort but the assault failed. Menéndez sailed 40 miles (64 km) south, built Fort Augustine, then attacked Fort Caroline again, killing 132 colonists and driving the French from the region. He renamed the place Fort San Mateo and continued establishing forts to the north to win Native American peace and Catholic converts.*

## THE NATCHEZ

During most of the European-provoked wars on the Indians, the Natchez and Taënsa of Mississippi, descendants of the Mexican-influenced Mississippian culture, lived in relative peace. Then, an expedition down the Mississippi by French explorer René-Robert de La Salle in 1682 brought white men into the region. By the turn of the eighteenth century, the French had established a colony along the Gulf Coast from New Orleans to Mobile. After a 1729 land swindle, the Natchez attacked a French fort and killed 300 colonists. The French and their Choctaw allies waged war against the Natchez; the few survivors were absorbed by sympathetic Chickasaw and Cherokee villages.

**BELOW** *Decoys were used among the tribes of Florida and elsewhere to attract small game. Using bark, feathers, and other materials they were practical handicraft projects for members of a number of tribes. This one, made of painted tule reeds and feathers, was discovered in Lovelock Cave, Nevada.*

# The French and Indian War

**T**he French and Indian War is the name given to the final struggle for control of North America that decided whether France or Britain would control the eastern part of the continent. It was the culmination of a series of conflicts fought in both the Old and New Worlds. France, with power in the hands of King Louis XV and his advisors, and Britain, with power shared between King George II and its constitutional government, dominated European politics. Their economic might and military and naval strength enabled them to colonize many parts of the world. Although there had been conflicts and treaties affecting North America before 1754, these were incidental to the global balance of power. The greatest change previously was that in 1713 a treaty transferred a large part of Nova Scotia to Britain from New France, the French colony that stretched from eastern Canada to the Great Lakes.

**ABOVE** *The defeat of a combined force of Indians, colonists, and British regulars under General Edward Braddock along the Monongahela River, July 9, 1755, on the approach to Fort Duquesne, was a tragic case of a leader ill-fitted to the role.*

〜〜〜 ☻ 〜〜〜

What was at stake in North America was trade with Native Americans. Even though these European powers derived more income from Caribbean sugar operations than from furs, tobacco, and other products imported from North America, the balance of power across the large continent was crucial to each empire. Key to success were the ties maintained with the Indian tribes with which they traded. The French had the advantage of starting earlier and establishing a network of modest posts and a few forts throughout the vast north and western regions, such as at Fort Detroit (1701.) With these they carried on the necessary commerce while posing no great threat to the Indians' homes and hunting grounds. The British provided the tribes with better quality and cheaper trade goods, but the constant flow of more settlers inland in the semi-autonomous colonies was of greater concern to the Indians.

War finally came to a head over a previously underutilized portion of the continent, the Ohio Valley. When English traders pushed west of the Appalachians

**Document**
ITEM 6. In the wars involving colonial expansion prior to the Seven Years' War, the British colonies were virtually left to defend themselves. This proclamation by the Lieutenant Governor of Massachusetts calls for colonists to hunt down Indians and offers a bounty for kill or capture. This desperate action was in response to French sanctioned raids by their Indian allies on New England colonies. **(See pocket page 31.)**

**ABOVE** *Benjamin Franklin created this eighteeenth-century political cartoon in his* Pennsylvania Gazette *on May 9, 1754. The woodcut accompanied an essay Franklin wrote urging unity among the bitterly divided colonies as the only way to assure that dangers from the French and their allies could be countered effectively. Franklin's overall political thinking was greatly influenced by the Iroquois leader Canassatego, who spoke at an Indian–British assembly in Philadelphia in 1744.*

**BELOW LEFT** *A woodcut diagram of the Battle of Lake George, fought near Lake George on September 8, 1755. Colonial troops and Native Americans under the British colonies' premier Indian agent, General William Johnson, defeated a force of French regulars, Canadians, and Indians under Jean-Armand Dieskau, the supreme French commander in Canada at the time.*

in the 1750s and discovered the network of rivers that fed the Ohio, they began to trade in the region, controlled by the powerful Iroquois alliance. Plans were made to build forts and settle the area. The French saw this as a threat to their vast trade network, from the Great Lakes region down the Mississippi Valley to New Orleans. The governor of New France was ordered to drive the British traders out. Both sides met with the tribes of the Ohio Valley to seek allies. The British made efforts to unite the separate colonies, form militia units, import regular soldiers, and firm up Indian alliances.

A fort was built by the British on a triangle of land where the Allegheny and Monongahela Rivers joined to form the Ohio, the gateway to the region. The war started in June 1754, when a young Virginia militia commander, George Washington, led a force with orders from the Governor of Virginia to retake the fort, which the French had seized. Washington's men, accompanied by Native American allies, fired on a French patrol, killing the commander. The incident led to a larger French force surrounding Washington's camp, called Fort Necessity, and then forcing the Virginians to surrender. Washington and most of his force were allowed to return Virginia, with Washington reporting to the governor in Williamsburg.

From this modest beginning, the two sides prepared for a major conflict. Britain's strong-willed Prime Minister, William Pitt, pushed for complete victory in America and mobilized a huge war effort. British regulars backed by artillery, colonial militia, and warriors from the Mohawk, Catawba, Creek, and Cherokee tribes faced off against French and Canadian forces and their Indian allies from the Catholicized Iroquois of Canada and Great Lakes tribes. The war was fought on two fronts, with a combination of sieges, formal battles, and guerrilla-style combat waged by small patrols in the undeveloped frontier. Both sides scored victories, with the British taking of Fort Duquesne (Pittsburgh) in 1758, Fort Niagara and Quebec in 1759, and Montreal (1760,) proving more decisive than French victories at Monongahela, Fort Oswego (1756,) Fort William Henry (1757,) and elsewhere.

In the end, with greater numbers of soldiers and a superior navy able to transport men and materiel across the Atlantic freely, while also blockading New France's resupply along their main water artery, the St. Lawrence River, the British won the war. The final peace treaty, signed in 1763, handed control over Canada to the British. Although not the only war fought between whites for colonial interests in which Native Americans participated, it was perhaps the one in which they fought in greatest numbers on both sides. One of the war's most devastating consequences for them was seeing the victor gain more of their land through increased post-war settlement between the Appalachian Mountains and the Mississippi River.

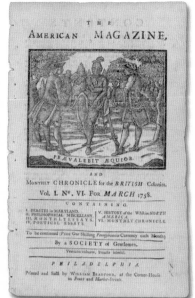

**ABOVE** The American Magazine, *published in Philadelphia, displayed on the cover of its March 1758 issue a woodcut of a Frenchman and an Englishman competing for the loyalty of a Native American standing between them leaning on a rifle. Praevalebit Aequior, meaning "The appropriate one will prevail," refers to the gift-giving that accompanied the recruitment of braves to fight for one side or the other.*

**ABOVE RIGHT** *Several tomahawk styles are displayed here. A leather wrapped stone makes the head of one, while pounded metal tops the other. Both are mounted on wooden handles as is the novel pipe tomahawk pictured below.*

**ABOVE** *The death of General Wolfe in the Battle of Quebec, September 1759. Though he found a way to overcome Quebec's strong natural defensive cliffs by funneling troops up a narrow path and onto the Plains of Abraham adjacent to Quebec's undefended west, General James Wolfe might have missed the chance for victory had not Louis Jordan, the Marquis de Montcalm, sent a fraction of his command outside Quebec's fortifications to meet him. The resulting battle caused the deaths of both commanders and the beginning of the end for the French and their Indian allies in the war.*

## TOMAHAWK

The tomahawk was probably the Native American weapon most feared during the French and Indian War. In the hands of a skilled warrior it could club or bash open the head of a victim or if thrown a short distance it could slice open a large gash. Originally tomahawks comprised a stone head, grooved in the middle and tied with hide strips to a notched stick. Under European influence, the stone heads were often replaced by pounded and sharpened metal. Some metal heads were bored out, and the implement doubled as a smoking receptacle, giving rise to the term pipe tomahawk.

**BACKGROUND** *In this engraving of a dramatic painting by Felix Octavius Carr Darley, the Marquis de Montcalm, the French general in command in Canada, is shown trying to stop Native Americans from attacking unarmed British and colonial soldiers leaving Fort William Henry in August 1757. Montcalm gave the defenders generous surrender terms, disappointing his Abnaki allies as he tried to prevent the eventual killing of nearly 200.*

# The California Mission System

**W**est of the Hohokam and Mogollón were members of the Desert Tradition that did not experience the extremes of climatic conditions endured by their neighbors to the east. Yet they practiced no agriculture, for their plant-based diets came from gathering. They are known as the Acorn People and until less than a century ago, similar primitive societies still existed in parts of Baja California. The Acorn People of Alta California lived primarily along the coast, from the current United States border with Mexico to the San Francisco Bay area, where a somewhat different culture began to appear.

〰〰 ⚚ 〰〰

The Acorn People did not subsist solely on the hard nuts of oak trees lining inland canyons and foothills, but it was the basis of a meal from which they derived their basic calorific needs. The potentially deadly tannic acid that prevents acorns from being a modern food was leached out after grinding. To supplement this staple, people gathered other wild grasses and roots, as well as insects, hunted deer and rabbit, and netted fish and clams. They lived in conical thatched grass houses, but spent most of the mild-weather months shielded by a reed roof supported by wooden poles. They wore very little clothing, made baskets and other woven utensils, and had simple belief systems. Their most involved ceremonies were the coming-of-age rituals. Of all these tribes, the Chumash were the only ones to exploit the sea fully, using crafted plank boats to navigate the island channels off the coast of their homeland near present-day Malibu, Ventura, and Santa Barbara.

The tribes of the Acorn People lived their lives unchanged in California for thousands of years. Then, in 1769, in an effort to expand their colonial power, the Spanish sent an expedition north to Alta California. Led by Father Junipero Serra, the Franciscan friars, backed by soldiers, began to establish missions. The first was Mission San Diego de Alcalá, and then San Carlos Borromeo, San Antonio de Padua, San Gabriel (near modern Los Angeles), and San Luis Obispo (in 1772.) The missions' purpose was to convert the natives to Christianity, and so the friars, aided by soldiers based in *presidios*

## FROM TRIBES TO BANDS

The transition of California's southern and central coast Indians from an independent lifestyle to the highly structured and disciplined life of the missions and back again was a shock to their cultures. Many died from European diseases to which they had no resistance, and the survivors suffered from the scattering of their population after secularization. Those that remained as communities sought refuge in the inland areas away from the rancheros and coastal developments. There they formed bands, practiced the agricultural techniques learned at the missions, and continued to produce outstanding basketry.

**LEFT** *J. Ed Bacon of Salinas photographed Old Gabriel, a Monterey Indian, about the turn of the twentieth century. His notes list the man as being 145 years old at the time and that he helped build the Carmel Mission. Construction for Mission San Carlos Borromeo de Carmelo was begun in 1770 and improvements would have gone on for years, so the claim may have merit.*

**BOTTOM LEFT** *Mission San Diego de Alcalá. This was the first mission founded in Alta California by Father Junipero Serra and was begun on July 16, 1769 at the Presidio overlooking San Diego Bay. The pictured mission building is the chapel of the second mission, built six miles (10 km) inland in 1774. It was used as a mission, military barracks, and church, and fell into great disrepair by the time of this 1904 photograph. A major reconstruction was begun in 1931.*

**BELOW** *A late-eighteenth-century illustration shows Native Americans and Catholic padres working together to build an unidentified mission. Missions continued to be built in isolated areas after secularization, as those Mission Indians who had undergone transformation were attracted to subsequent missionary ventures by a handful of friars.*

LEFT *Petroglyphs at Sloan Canyon, Nevada. A trove of intricate petroglyphs by people of the Desert Tradition was discovered at Sloan Canyon in the southern Nevada desert in the early twentieth century.*

(forts) nearby, drove the Indians from their homes and into the missions.

These Native Americans then underwent a transformation, both physically and spiritually. They were dressed in Spanish-inspired cotton attire, were taught to farm and make pottery, and, of course, instructed in the rigid religious beliefs of the Franciscans. Previously married couples were allowed to share small huts, but the rest of the tribe's people were segregated by sexes and occupied dormitory-style buildings. The missions were set up around an open courtyard and most daily activities—prayer, instruction, meals, and some of the work—were carried out within the courtyard. Continued building expanded the compounds, and eventually most contained an outer wall.

The Indians were well treated, but discipline was harsh. Some individuals escaped, but with their villages destroyed by the soldiers, they had nowhere to go, and a number of those who fled returned to the missions. Gradually, over the next 50 years, the mission system grew to include 21 separate missions, with the last, San Francisco Solano, built at Sonoma and completed in 1823, to stem the tide of Russian influence flowing down from the north. Although there were cases of violence, such as a massacre of Franciscans by rebellious Indians at Mission San Diego de Alcalá (on November 5, 1775,) most of the members of the Mission Indian tribes just endured the strict mission life and some actually benefited from their experiences.

BELOW *A Chumash metate (grinding surface) and mano (muller.) A Chumash woman would roll the metate over the mano to produce corn meal.*

BOTTOM RIGHT
*Chumash pictographs in the mountains of Malibu, California, tell the tale in pictures of the journey of Don Gaspár de Portolá through the area in November 1769.*

## The California Mission System

Sacramento R.

San Joaquin R.

Sonoma ⊕ San Francisco Solano
San Rafael ⊕ San Rafael Arcangel
San Francisco ⊕ San Francisco de Asís
⊕ San José
Santa Clara de Asís ● San Jose
Santa Cruz ⊕ ● Santa Cruz
⊕ San Juan Bautista
Carmel ⊕ Nuestra Señora de la Soledad
San Carlos Borromeo ⊕ ● Soledad
de Carmelo
San Antonio de Padua ⊕
⊕ San Miguel Arcángel
Paso Robles ●
San Luis Obispo ⊕ San Luis Obispo de Tolosa
Santa Maria ●
La Purisima Concepción ⊕ Santa Inés ⊕
Santa Bárbara
Santa Barbara ● ⊕ San Buenaventura
Ventura ● San Fernando Rey de España ⊕
Los Angeles ● San Fernando ●
San Gabriel Arcángel ⊕
San Juan Capistrano ●
San Juan Capistrano ⊕
San Luis Rey de Francia ⊕
San Luis Rey ●
San Diego de Alcalá ⊕
San Diego ●

Pacific Ocean

⊕ Mission Names
∙∙∙∙∙ Original Route of the Padres

0 — 100 kms
0 — 50 mls

## SECULARIZATION AND EMANCIPATION

In 1834, the California missions were secularized by the newly independent Mexican government. Unsure of the loyalty of the powerful Franciscans in Alta California and sensitive to pressure from the owners of huge ranches there, the secularization reduced the church's political clout. The Mission Indians were freed from the control of the friars. Since many had been born and raised on the missions, the adjustment to freedom was a profound shock. Many ended up in indentured servitude on the ranches, but others who did not formed into communities again. The Emancipation Proclamation of California Tribes was a unified statement that reaffirmed the freedom of the Acorn People's descendants.

# Russian Influence in the Northwest

**T**he Eskimos, Aleuts, and other tribes of the Arctic and sub-Arctic regions of North America were the last to emigrate from Asia, but some of them were the very first to encounter Europeans. In late tenth century, on the icy coast of Greenland, a Norseman named Erik the Red led an expedition across the Northern Atlantic and founded the first European settlement in the New World. A few Norsemen made it as far west as Labrador. The colony and the Eskimos who inhabited the region had little to do with each other. Then, in the twelfth century, the climate became colder, more Eskimos migrated to the region, and the Norse colonists either died, were murdered, or were absorbed into the native tribes. Virtually no trace of their journey to the sub-continent of Greenland exists, save some written records and recent archeological finds. It would be another 300 years before the Greenlanders and the rest of the Eskimos' fascinating culture would be disturbed by the white man's influence.

To the Eskimos that inhabited the region near and beyond the Arctic Circle, the harsh climate was something that required only slight adaptation from the life in their assumed original homeland of Siberia a mere 3,000 years earlier. Along with the Aleuts and the inland Eyak, they ranged across approximately the upper third of the continent. Their language base in the west was Athapaskan, in the east, Algonquian. Their diet was, with few exceptions, totally carnivorous, and traditionally hunting was the main occupation for males, with some assistance from the women. The game for the inland Eyak tribes included the mammals that roamed the tundra; bears, moose, oxen, and, most importantly, caribou. Migrating birds in the summer and fish supplemented their diet and provided for many other needs. The Aleuts, living on the wooded islands that once formed the land bridge, hunted smaller mammals, game birds, and fish, netted or snared with lines and hooks.

**LEFT** *A summer sealskin tent with an old Eskimo woman sitting outside at Point Barrow, Alaska. These dwellings were constructed for the short summer season, anchored on poles of willow or driftwood and held down against strong winds by rocks.*

**ABOVE RIGHT** *Diagram of an igloo interior.*

**Document**

ITEM 7. Russian Aleut Primer. The Russian church in America strove to retain native languages and use them to communicate their religious teachings. Father Ioann Veniaminov created an alphabet for the Aluet language, and aided by the Aleut Toien (Chief), wrote this primer in 1845.
(See pocket page 31.)

## THE IGLOO

Another Eskimo invention was the igloo, or ice house. These domed habitats were constructed of packed snow bricks, carefully built up for integral support, and placed on frozen ice flows for temporary or long-term winter shelter. More permanent styles could contain several interconnected rooms and storage areas. Windows were made from ice sheets or seal innards, and an exhaust hole in the top carried away fumes and smoke. With a frozen condensation layer formed by the temperature difference, the occupants could be quite comfortable inside with little or no clothing. In the summer, seal-skin tents replaced the igloos for shelter. A skilled Eskimo could construct a temporary igloo on the hunt in less than an hour.

**LEFT** *Mrs. Kleinschmidt, the wife of the photographer, was a dinner guest of the Eskimo family inside their igloo in this 1913 photograph. They all wore traditional dress and dined on frozen crabs. Among the family's possessions visible in the picture are snow shoes and a coiled rope.*

**BELOW** *This harpoon and tether is attributed to the Clayquot tribe of the west coast of Vancouver Island, British Columbia. The point is made of antler.*

Along coastal Alaska and the Arctic areas of northwestern Canada, whaling was also practiced, not just as a symbol of male prowess—on which the Nootka set great store—but as a source of food, oil, clothing, and construction materials. The whales, primarily beluga and white, were tracked by teams in open boats called umiaks, then harpooned and speared as the animals tired. Sometimes whales could be caught while breeding in inlet waters.

The Eskimos, who inhabited the upper reaches of Canada and Alaska, had one predominant prey, the seal. Of tantamount importance to their survival was seal oil, which, when burned in stone bowls, provided light and warmth in a land almost totally devoid of any kind of timber. Just as the Plains Indians used virtually every part of the bison, so too the Eskimos found practical uses for every bit of the seal's body. In a culture without organized religion, the Eskimos would perform a ritual after killing to release the animal's spirit.

When European influence returned to the region, it was at first fully exploitative, and later a dash of paternalism was added to the exploitation. Russian traders came to Alaska and the west coast in search of ivory and fur between 1740 and 1765. The Tsar of Russia stepped in toward the end of the eighteenth century and required chartered fur and whaling companies to bring Orthodox missionaries to the New World as an obligatory part of their teams. Churches and schools became common in the Aleutian Islands and many converts were counted among those who survived the diseases introduced by the foreigners. On the Alaskan mainland, the missionaries met with more resistance. From the other direction, the Hudson's Bay Company, which had a virtual monopoly over the fur trade throughout most of Canada and beyond, quickly realized the practicality of looking after its Native American trappers with education and other social programs. As Canada formed a more independent government, these commercial efforts were replaced by provincial programs, and peace and order were brought to a lawless area with the establishment of the Royal Canadian Mounted Police in 1873.

**TOP LEFT** *This photograph shows the process of drying salmon at the Aleut village of Old Harbor, Alaska in 1889. The relatively mild climate of the Aleutian Islands afforded the natives a wider range of fish species for food to augment plant foods, birds, seals, and other mammals.*

**RIGHT** *A Tlingit fishing camp of wooden A-frame huts at Lituya Bay, Alaska is pictured in this 1786 engraving. The village, called Port of France by the French naval officer who sketched it, was established by the inhabitants for the fishing season.*

## THE KAYAK

The kayak, a skin-covered, sleek watercraft, was an Eskimo invention which neighboring tribes adapted. The true Eskimo kayak was pointed at bow and stern, made of cured sealskin stretched on a whalebone or driftwood frame, and ranged in size up to the most common, 18 feet (5.5 metres). It was a one-man boat. With clothing attached to the small round opening amidships, the complete package was watertight. Capsizing was not a problem and the craft could be easily righted with the double-ended paddle—another Eskimo invention—used to propel the kayak.

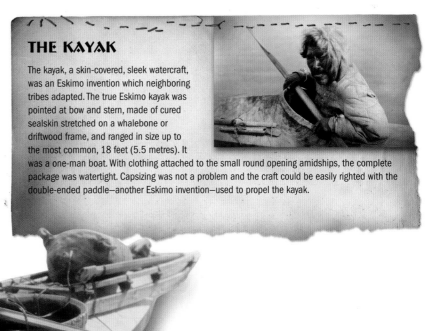

**LEFT** *This kayak equipped for seal hunting belonged to an Eskimo from Nunivak Island, Alaska. Among the hunting items shown are harpoons and a float made from seal intestines.*

# The New Nation and the Original Inhabitants

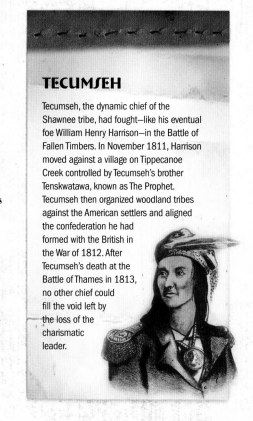

After the United States gained its independence from Great Britain, the governing bodies of the new nation turned their attention to other sources of conflict. These were domestic issues brought on by the westward expansion of white settlements. King George III had declared the Appalachian Mountains to be the boundary of the colonies, while the land to the west was considered the sovereign territory of the Native American tribes. However, long before Cornwallis met with defeat at Yorktown in 1781, white settlers were pressing beyond that frontier and carving out farms on Indian land. Though some eastern and southeast tribes fought for the American Revolution—including members of the Oneida, Tuscarora, and Cauhnawaga tribes who fought with the Continental Army at Saratoga—many Native Americans viewed the United States and its infant government with distrust, even hostility.

The new federal government adopted a policy of pacification in its relations with the Native Americans. George Washington's administration set up government trading houses, in Washington's words, to "conciliate the Indians' attachment." It was more of a political maneuver rather than an economic one. The idea was to keep the tribes as small independent entities under the protection of the federal government. In 1786, the Treaty of Hopewell between the federal government and the Cherokees, Choctaws, and Chickasaws set boundaries for Indian lands and established laws to protect Indian sovereignty. But encroachment by settlers continued.

Native American animosity toward the government increased in the region affected by the Northwest Ordinance of 1787, which created the Northwest Territory, and established a procedure by which states could be created out of the western settlements. The tribes in what are now Ohio, Indiana, Illinois, Wisconsin, and Michigan preferred British and French trappers and trading companies over the frontier farmers of the United States. The white settlers' approach to the Native Americans was generally one of lawlessness. Tribal settlements and individual Indians were treated roughly or violently. In 1791, Native Americans armed by British individuals attacked settlements in the Northwest Territories, and a group of U.S. soldiers was attacked and scattered near the Wabash River in Ohio.

Washington issued a warning to the Native American tribes in a series of proclamations in 1794. Later that year, on August 20, an army under General Anthony Wayne defeated a force of braves at Fallen Timbers, Ohio, ending resistance in the region for a time. The Treaty of Greenville signed in 1795 with the chiefs of 12 tribes, including the Shawnee, Miami, and Ottawa, ceded most of Ohio to the United States.

Trouble began again in 1799, as settlers began to move into new Mississippi Territory, created a year earlier. As the nineteenth century began, new developments increased the threats posed to the Native American population. The Louisiana Purchase in 1803 more than doubled the territory of the United States. Additional roads and trails, and the invention of the steam engine for rail and water travel, made settlement easier.

**BELOW** *This fanciful nineteenth-century lithograph of the American victory shows the death of Tecumseh and a mounted William Henry Harrison leading a charge In the Battle of Thames, at Malden, Ontario, October 5, 1813.*

**Document**
ITEM 8. Proclamation, dated December 12, 1792, describing an act of violence against a Cherokee village in Georgia and offering a reward for justice. It is an example of Washington's policy of extending federal protection to the Native American tribes as entities within a larger nation. It is signed be the President and Secretary of State, Thomas Jefferson.
(See pocket page 31.)

**ABOVE LEFT** *Though he himself was a Shawnee chief, Billy Shane fought against his tribesmen, who were aligned with the British in the War of 1812. He was wounded in the Battle of Thames, Ontario, Canada.*

**LEFT** *By the time George Washington became the first American President he had already dealt with Native Americans as a military commander in two wars. He took cautious control of Indian affairs in the new nation through trade, treaties, and military action.*

President Thomas Jefferson recommended that the tribes east of the Mississippi move to new open territory west of the river. Under Chief Justice John Marshall's leadership, the U.S. Supreme Court invalidated the 1763 boundary line established by the British king, George III, and upheld states' claims to Native American lands.

Conflict returned to the Northwest Territory. In 1811, William Henry Harrison, then Governor of Indiana Territory, defeated Native Americans at Tippecanoe Creek in the western part of the state. The Northwest Territory tribes then joined the British in the War of 1812 in a confederation led by Shawnee Chief Tecumseh. Harrison led United States soldiers in defeating the British in the Battle of Thames, Ontario, in 1813. Tecumseh was killed in the battle and the Native American confederacy in the northwest collapsed.

Complementing this muscular approach to Indian affairs was a paternalistic side. In 1816, Governor Lewis Cass of Michigan Territory and William Clark, of the future Lewis and Clark expedition, drew up a series of regulations recognizing a moral obligation to care for Native Americans. The result was a framework of dependency that called for programs for the Native American population, while at the same time forcing them off their lands. New treaties signed by the Creeks and Cherokee caused them to forfeit much of their land.

The U.S. government policy of relocation also affected tribes in the Northwest Territories. Though they signed a treaty in 1804 that allowed for coexistence with whites, the Sauk (Sac) and Fox tribes were forced out of Illinois and west of the Mississippi. In 1832, under Chief Black Hawk, the Sauks returned to Illinois to plant crops. Violence erupted and the Black Hawk War ended with a massacre of tribesmen at Bad Axe River in Wisconsin. By 1850, nearly all Native Americans east of the Mississippi were on reservations.

**LEFT** *Anthony Wayne was a veteran general who scored key victories in the Revolutionary War. President Washington put him in charge of an expedition in 1794 to quell disturbances by Native Americans armed by sympathetic Englishmen in the Northwest Territories.*

**BELOW** *This copper peace medal bearing the likeness of Thomas Jefferson in an 1801 design was given to Powder Face, a Cheyenne chief. These medals were freely given by the U.S. government in conjunction with treaty negotiations. Many of the chiefs painted by the mid-nineteenth-century painters are posed wearing peace medals.*

## BLACK HAWK

Black Hawk's uneventful death on an Iowa reservation in 1838 belied his tumultuous life. He was a Sauk war chief who resented the American government, yet also cautioned against bringing on war. In 1831, he was forced to lead his people west across the Mississippi and sign a treaty banning their return. Challenged by young warriors, he led the Sauks back to their former Illinois planting grounds in 1832. Though he won the battle of Stillman's Run, Black Hawk, failing to receive support from other tribes, lost most of his followers, including those slaughtered at the Battle of Bad Axe River. Captured, Black Hawk was held up as an example to keep the region peaceful.

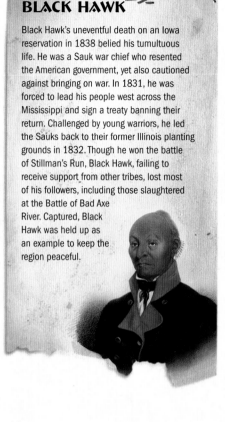

*" I believe the Indian then to be in body and mind equal to the Whiteman "*

**Thomas Jefferson**

**BELOW LEFT** *The meeting of Tecumseh and William Henry Harrison at Vincennes, the capital of Indiana Territory, in 1809 is portrayed in this lithograph. Tecumseh was angered over the Treaty of Fort Wayne, signed by a number of tribes and chiefs, which ceded 2.5 million acres of Ohio and Indiana to the United States. Tecumseh assured Harrison his followers were not at war with the U.S. then left on a journey to spread his message of resistance to the tribes of the southeast.*

**BELOW** *Karl Bodmer created this image of Sac (Sauk) and Fox Indians during his trip to the U.S. with German Prince Maximilian, a naturalist and budding ethnologist with a great interest in studying Native Americans. Most likely Bodmer sketched these warriors while accompanying Chief Keokuk to St. Louis on a mission to free the imprisoned Black Hawk.*

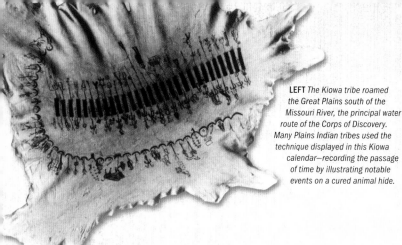

## AMERICAN BISON

When Lewis and Clark came upon the Great Plains west of the Mississippi River, they encountered vast herds of bison. Lacking horses, they themselves did not hunt the animal but the nomadic tribes of the plains, the Cheyenne, Lakota, Shoshone, Yanktonai, Crow, and others, did. Bison provided nearly everything the members of these tribes needed to live. The eastern Siouan cultures had gradually abandoned agriculture when the adoption of the horse gave them greater mobility to chase the bison. Indian and white hunters nearly exhausted the American bison herds by the beginning of the twentieth century and now only a few remain, all of them in captivity or on preserves.

# Native Americans Encountered by Lewis and Clark

B y the beginning of the nineteenth century, the administration of President Thomas Jefferson was faced with a diplomatic crisis involving New Orleans and French designs on Spanish Florida. Napoleon Bonaparte, focused on financing a planned war against Great Britain, not only offered to sell New Orleans to the United States, but the entire Louisiana Territory as well. For 15 million dollars (plus 5 million to settle naval claims,) the Jefferson administration bought 858,000 square miles of land. Jefferson was interested in having the northwest portion of the North American continent explored even before the purchase, and had secretly charged his private secretary, Meriwether Lewis, with preparing an expedition for that purpose. Lewis asked his former superior, William Clark, an experienced frontiersman, to share leadership of what would become known as the Corps of Discovery, made up of army men and civilian volunteers. In late 1803, they sailed for St. Louis, made winter camp near the mouth of the Missouri River, and finalized preparations.

ᗯᗯᗯ ⚲ ᗯᗯᗯ

LEFT *Mato-Tope was a chief of the Mandan tribe when he was painted by both George Catlin and Karl Bodmer on their western journeys. He was himself an enthusiastic artist and connected well with the two painters. In this Bodmer watercolor Mato-Tope wears his finest garments and carries a lance decorated with an Arikara scalp. The Arikara warrior killed Mato-Tope's brother and the chief avenged the act by slaying him with this lance.*

BELOW *Three Cheyenne warriors overlook the Great Plains in a photograph by Edward Curtis. The Cheyenne, along with the Lakota (Teton Sioux,) once controlled the Great Plains hunting grounds north of the Arkansas River in what are now western Kansas, Colorado, Wyoming, and southern Montana. But disease, settlement, and military action by the United States government greatly diminished their numbers and power.*

BELOW *Meriwether Lewis and William Clark meet a council of Native Americans from an unspecified tribe in this illustration from an 1810 publication of the journals of the Corps of Discovery.*

Key among Jefferson's objectives for the Corps of Discovery was to establish friendly relations with the dozens of Native American tribes Lewis and Clark would encounter on their journey. Those tribes in the immediate area of the Mississippi, such as the Osage, Quapaw, Fox, and Sauks, were already familiar with Americans as a result of frontier trade conducted along the Mississippi. On May 14, 1804, the 43-man expedition began the ascent of the Missouri River in three boats, two flat-bottom canoes and a keel-boat. The plan was to ascend the Missouri River as far as the Rockies, then portage the craft across the mountains to the Columbia river, which English sea explorers had discovered during their voyages in the northern Pacific.

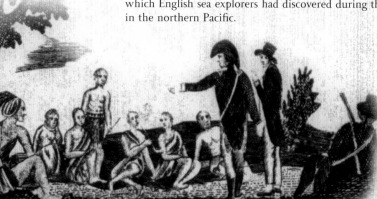

## SACAJAWEA

Sacajawea, a Shoshone, was captured as a teenager by a Hidatsa war party and sold to French Canadian trapper Toussaint Charbonneau, who married her. In the spring of 1805, when Charbonneau was hired by Lewis and Clark for their expedition to the Rocky Mountains and beyond, Sacajawea and their infant son went along. She proved to be an invaluable guide for the expedition. When they reached a Shoshone village, she was reunited with her brother, Cameahwait, the village chief. Sacajawea acted as an interpreter for Lewis and Clark and helped them obtain horses from her brother's tribe. She accompanied the expedition to the Pacific Ocean and on the return east to a Mandan village, where she and her family bade goodbye to the great explorers.

In July, the expedition began to enter uncharted territory. On the eastern edge of the great prairie lands of present-day Nebraska and Iowa they attempted to make contact with a known tribe, the Pawnee, but they were away on their annual buffalo hunt. Lewis and Clark then encountered previously undiscovered Native Americans, Oto, Missouri, and Arikaras tribesmen. The interpreter in the Corps of Discovery communicated with these Indians in sign language, and despite this inexact method, no major points were lost in communication. The expedition then encountered the Lakota, the first tribe openly unfriendly to the expedition. The Lakota had a proud tradition as bison hunters and warriors. They demanded tribute from Lewis and Clark for passing across their hunting grounds. A stand-off ensued, but the expedition moved on without a major incident. They made their first winter quarters of the journey at the camp of the Mandan, and also visited the neighboring Hidatsa tribe.

Here they copied their notes on the expedition; Lewis was primarily concerned with the scientific discoveries of the trip, Clark with its geographical exploration. In the spring, the keel-boat and a group of the soldiers returned to St. Louis with journals and samples of the expedition's discoveries to date. Lewis and Clark hired a French Canadian to join the expedition, Toussaint Charbonneau, who brought his Shoshonean bride, Sacajawea, and their infant son with him. Lewis and Clark were reluctant to have a woman and papoose on the rugged journey, but Sacajawea's aid proved to be invaluable to the expedition.

In late spring, they encountered the foothills of the Rockies, began the ascent on foot, and then came to a Shoshonean village. Obtaining horses, they crossed the mountains, and in October met the friendly Nez Percé, who told of a water passage westward. Building new, smaller canoes, the party navigated the western Rockies via the Clearwater and Snake rivers and arrived at the mouth of the Columbia River before the onset of winter. They built a fort on the Pacific Coast, but failed to make much progress in striking trade negotiations with

the coastal tribes, who had been trading with European sailing expeditions for decades. With the coming of spring, the expedition, having failed to make contact with any American vessel on the Pacific coast, returned over the mountains, exploring different routes part of the way, and returned to a heroes' welcome in St. Louis. Although the Corps of Discovery achieved their goals of exploration and negotiating peaceful trade pacts, they also unwittingly opened the door for the massive western settlement that would forever change the Native American cultures of the Great Plains and beyond.

ABOVE *This illustration shows a buffalo hunt in progress in an area in the shadow of the Rocky Mountains. The bison herds decreased rapidly in the nineteenth century through the combination of Indian and white hunters, and prairie trails and farms that disrupted their migration patterns.*

BELOW LEFT *A camp of Piegans, one of three bands of the Blackfeet tribes, at Fort McKenzi, Montana. Karl Bodmer (who painted this) and Prince Maximillian stayed at this fur-trading post for the entire month of August, 1833.*

ABOVE *In 1833 Bodmer created this watercolor of a Mandan looking up at a sacred shrine. The two poles represented the Creator and the Woman Who Never Dies, the former a shrine to the Giver of Life, and the latter the eternal provider of subsistence to the tribe. The shrine protected a Mandan village's burial site.*

BELOW *This illustration of the interior of a Dakota tipi by P. Rindisbacher shows a group of Indians and a white man, probably a soldier or trader, smoking pipes. Smoking the ceremonial pipe was an element of diplomacy on the plains and could signify peace and agreement. But pipes were also smoked as a prelude to warfare.*

# Indian Bureaus and the First Reservations

**W**hen Thomas Jefferson proclaimed the Indians were equals to the white man in every way, he secretly hoped this equality would be practiced mainly in the lands west of the Mississippi River. Like many of his contemporaries, he did not suppose that the incorporation of Native Americans into the burgeoning white settlements of the east would be a smooth transition. Though the British treaty on Indian sovereignty was struck down by the United States Supreme Court under Chief Justice John Marshall, the decision would not be Marshall's final word on the subject.

The American president who was most fervent in pushing for a policy of Indian "removal" (as it was then termed) was Andrew Jackson. His interest in white expansion was demonstrated by his actions in Florida beginning in 1817. In sharing Jefferson's secret views, Jackson was far more vocal on the subject. Indian Affairs received bureau-level status in the executive branch before Jackson's presidency, however he was the first to use the spreading influence of Indian agents to secure pacts which drove Native Americans from their homelands.

While some of the eastern tribes, already virtually decimated by disease and conflict, gave in to the establishment of the reservation system, those in the Old Northwest did not. After the Indians of Ohio, Indiana, Michigan, and Illinois lost their homelands by, among other reasons, backing the British in the War of 1812, they were driven to the west side of the Mississippi, or to the area of the river's source in what are now the states of Wisconsin and Minnesota.

In the south, the situation was different. Those tribes that suffered most in squabbles between themselves and with the white man, such as the Tutelo, Catawba, and Pamunkey, found their surviving members reduced to living on reservations that represented a tiny portion of the lands they had once controlled. However, further south resistance to removal was more prevalent. Particularly well organized in their objections were the Cherokee, whose territory once covered much of western North Carolina, Tennessee, northeast Alabama, and northwest Georgia. In 1795, they signed a treaty that greatly reduced their holdings and confined the Cherokee Nation to an area encompassing northwest Georgia and small parts of Tennessee and Alabama. The capital of their well-educated and, for the most part, prosperous

**ABOVE** *Karl Bodmer, one of the European artists who traveled throughout the United States in the first part of the nineteenth century painting Native Americans with his employer and expedition chronicler, Prince Maximilian, painted the detailed watercolor in this lithograph. The subjects are from left, a Missouri Indian, an Oto Indian, and a chief of the Poncas, who is wearing a large American peace medal. Bodmer painted on-site and whether or not he got these three individuals to pose together, they were probably painted in 1833 as Maximilian and Bodmer traveled the Missouri River on the riverboat Yellowstone.*

## OSCEOLA

Osceola was the son of a Creek woman, a member of the "Red Sticks" portion of the Creek nation who fled to Florida after the defeat at Horseshoe Bend. He grew to the status of an elite warrior among the fugitives and gained the trust and respect of the Seminoles who had long established a home in Florida. When he became chief he incurred the wrath of Andrew Jackson by accepting runaway slaves into the tribe's fold. Jackson used the tenets of the Runaway Slave laws as legal justification to wage war on the Seminoles after Osceola rejected a removal treaty that offered the tribe only two cents an acre for their land. Osceola and his warriors—including some African Americans—eluded United States troops for two years until he was captured in the fall of 1837. Osceola died in captivity at Fort Moultrie, South Carolina, in 1838, but the Seminoles carried on the fight until defeated in this, the Second Seminole War, in 1842.

**TOP** *This Indian encampment in Louisiana was painted by François Bernard in 1860. The artists of the romantic period portrayed the Native Americans as integral to the landscape, in natural harmony with their surroundings. Choctaw villages on the north shore of Lake Pontchartrain survived the mass removal to Indian Territory. Other small villages dotted the Mississippi River.*

**ABOVE LEFT** *A bison at rest on the Great Plains. Though many thousands of animals roamed the prairie at the beginning of the nineteenth century, the number dwindled to hundreds by the end of the century. At that time, a new processing technique created a demand for their hide as a leather source, so white "hide men" killed thousands. This action also deterred free-roaming plains tribes from hunting bison off the reservation and greatly contributed to pushing the animal toward extinction.*

**LEFT** *Abraham Quary was listed as the last of the Nantucket tribe in this lithograph of an 1834 sketch by Jerome Thompson. He posed for Thompson on Nantucket Island when he was a 64-year-old chief.*

**BELOW** *Fort Laramie, pictured here in a late-nineteenth-century photograph, began as a trading post on the Oregon Trail and in 1849 was converted to an army outpost. Here, in 1851, a landmark peace treaty was arranged by Indian Agent Thomas Fitzpatrick and signed by chiefs of eight major northern plains tribes. It provided for the peaceful passage of settlers and traders and divided hunting grounds along tribal lines.*

population was New Echota. They continued to refine their culture and shape their national republic after the model of the United States.

By the time Andrew Jackson came to power in 1829, the landscape had changed, literally. Not only were white settlers taking over Cherokee lands, with a small find of gold complicating matters, but the State of Georgia had passed laws making it almost impossible for the Cherokee to maintain control of their land. The tribe challenged the law in the federal court system and this time Justice Marshall used a case involving two U.S. citizens arrested for helping the Cherokee, to rule (in February 1832) in favor of the Indians and strike down the Georgia law. But Jackson made it clear he would not use federal government resources to enforce the decision. Land violations continued unabated and, more seriously, the Cherokee council split into two factions: those resigned to removal to a new federal Indian Territory north of the Red River, and those who insisted on standing their ground.

The first of the Cherokee left Georgia in 1835, while others held out until 1838 when federal troops were called in to enforce the removal, made official by the Indian Removal Act of 1830 that established the Indian Territory. Those that held out to the end not only lost many of their possessions, they also suffered privations when they were rounded up and held in temporary stockades before being boarded on steamers for their new homes. Once there, they were not only forced to compete for prime land with those Cherokees who had left Georgia earlier, but also with three other relocated tribes, the Choctaw, Chickasaw, and Creeks. The Cherokees called the difficult and deadly journey the "Trail of Tears." The last of the Five Civilized Tribes—as they were known in the mid-nineteenth century—to arrive in Indian Territory were the Seminoles, who fought the United States in military actions initiated by Jackson and termed the Second and Third Seminole Wars (1835–42 and 1855–58.) Under their leaders Osceola, and others, the Seminoles of Florida were the last of the major tribes east of the Mississippi to be forced onto reservations or out of their homelands entirely.

**BELOW** *Seven mounted Spokane men look over a tributary of their namesake river in this Edward Curtis photograph. The tribe was later confined to the small Spokane Reservation in northeast Washington.*

**BELOW LEFT** *Fort Union was established in 1829 on the Missouri River near the mouth of the Yellowstone River, along what today is the North Dakota–Montana border. It was originally a trading post and in its early years was the westernmost outpost of Euro-American culture on the Missouri. Blackfeet and Assiniboins came to trade here.*

## INDIAN AGENTS

In 1789 the federal government established an arm of the War Department to deal with the Indians, but in 1824 Secretary of War John C. Calhoun reorganized the Indian Department into a separate entity, the Bureau of Indian Affairs. By that time, Indian agents, such as Albert Pike shown here, were already in the field, negotiating the deals and treaties that forced tribes to move onto reservations. The agents then issued the monetary awards, annual stipends, and supplies to the tribes, operating from established offices or agencies. While some individual agents crusaded for fair treatment, most simply carried out the insensitive policies established in Washington to herd Indians onto increasingly smaller tracts of land.

## SARAH WINNEMUCCA

Sarah was the daughter of a Northern Paiute chief, and was educated at a California women's college. She became an interpreter and scout and married a U.S. Army officer. In 1878, the Bannocks of Idaho waged a short war with the army, and the Northern Paiutes were considering joining their ranks. Sarah foresaw the destructive effect a war with the well-organized U.S. Army force would bring, and traveled between the lines to convince her father and his warriors not to go into battle. She was abandoned by her first officer husband but married another officer and later in life founded a school for Indian children.

# Gold and Settlers Challenge California Tribes

Like their neighbors to the south, the Native American tribes of northern and inland central California, as well as those Desert Tradition tribes between the Sierra Nevada and Rocky Mountains, seldom resorted to violence or intertribal warfare to settle disputes. This was primarily because there were fewer members of each tribe and the sparseness of the populations made the kind of political organization and tribal rivalry issues that bring on warfare untenable. The tribes were also skilled basket-makers, engaged in elaborate coming-of-age rituals and did not participate in any kind of agriculture.

**ABOVE LEFT** *Residents of the Round Valley Reservation pose in front of the Agency Office and Sutler Store in 1876. The northern California federal farm was one of seven established shortly after California became a state to force Indians off their ancestral lands for gold mining and other forms of white economic exploitation. The reservation brought together Yokuts, Pomos, and members of other tribes who were unaccustomed to living together.*

**RIGHT** *Edward Curtis called this misty scene* Smokey Day at the Sugar Bowl. *The northern California Hupa man is fishing with a wooden spear, a common method of catching salmon and other stream fish in the Trinity River Hupa homeland.*

There were, however, sharp differences between those tribes living on or near the coast and those east of the Sierra Nevada, especially in the means of acquiring food. It was only the coming of the white man that would give these groups a common cause. Those on the coastal plain, the Hupa, Pomo, Yuki tribes, and others, enjoyed abundant opportunities for gathering wild plant foods and fishing. Rivers flowed freely in Northern California and fish were speared or netted there to supplement the gathering of mollusks and other sea creatures. Even sea mammals, such as the sea lion and otter, were trapped and used for food and clothing. Some tribes hunted in the mountain foothills.

For those tribes to the east, the Mono, Washo, Paiute, and others, the arid conditions which prevailed for most of the year made food gathering more difficult. The rivers and streams fed by the eastern Sierra Nevada snowcap and other ranges allowed some fishing. A large variety of mammals were hunted. For those to the east, however, the desert conditions forced the women to seek out edible seeds and roots, and harvest insects; while the men went after the small mammals and reptiles that made the desert home, particularly the jackrabbit. All desert creatures were hunted except the coyote, an animal considered sacred by the Paiute and other tribes of the desert.

**LEFT** *Winnemucca, the Paiute Chief of western Nevada and father of Sarah Winnemucca, poses for a photographer in 1880. Winnemucca was the son-in-law and successor of Paiute chief Jack Truckee, a friend of whites who fought the Spanish in California alongside John C. Frémont. Winnemucca tried to maintain tribal lands and keep the peace, but anxious warriors under Numaga battled settlers at Pyramid Lake in 1860. Violence, mining, and settlers forced the tribe from Pyramid Lake into an inhospitable desert.*

ABOVE *This 1874 photograph shows a Uintah Ute in full war dress and a youth carrying a large decorated shoulder bag on their traditional mounts, ponies. By the late 1800s the Uintah were forced onto a desolate reservation in eastern Utah. After a short war in 1879 their close kin, the White River Utes of western Colorado, were forced onto the reservation as well.*

ABOVE *These Indian scouts pictured at the lava beds in central California were part of a military force sent in pursuit of Captain Jack and his Modoc band in 1873. Eadweard Muybridge, creator of this photograph, was a pioneer in using the camera for the study of human anatomy.*

## POMO BASKETRY ARTISTS

Many Native American cultures made and used baskets (a general classification for containers constructed of grass or plant fiber,) but the women of the Pomo tribe on the central Californian coast have been judged the finest by archeologists and anthropologists who have studied their work. They used both twining and coiling techniques with geometric patterns in a soothing rhythm. The containers were made in many different designs, with unusually shaped examples used for rituals. The baskets were often decorated with the colorful shells of abalone to give them a truly unique appearance.

As with the Mission Indians, the coming of the white man changed lifestyles which had endured for several millennia. Except for a few tribes impacted by the northern string of missions and seaside ports along the coast, the storm clouds would come from the east, in the form of settlers and, from 1849, gold and silver prospectors and those that followed in their wake.

In 1848, while constructing a sawmill on the American River, John Marshall, a foreman on a tract of land owned by John Sutter, discovered gold flakes in the water while the mill race was being constructed. After a trip to the provincial capital of Monterey to authenticate and file the claim, Sutter quickly changed the purpose of his property to mining. He had built a fort to protect his property near present-day Sacramento, but that was not enough to keep his land and Indian land free from hundreds of gold-seekers, squatting along the rivers and tributaries to pan gold from the silt-laden waters. Finds of gold, and particularly silver, in underground veins led prospectors to Nevada as well. Finally, the pilgrimage of another persecuted people, the Mormons, led to the establishment of a large colony in Utah from 1847, completing the incursion of whites into the lands of the Desert Tradition.

The impact on the Indians was immediate and tragic. Many were pressed into the service of the prospectors as indentured servants. Others found their prime fishing areas and gathering spots spoiled by the damming streams and the rapid building of boomtowns. The Indians here lacked the warrior tradition of the neighboring plains tribes, and were poorly prepared to fight for their homelands. The United States government quickly made the area, won in a decisive victory over Mexico in 1848, into the states of California in 1850, then Nevada in 1864. The Indians could only stand aside and watch with sadness the devastating effects of the "Gold Rush." One of the exceptions, however, was an 1862 attack on settlers in California's Owens Valley, east of the Sierra Nevada, in which United States troops were called out to put down the uprising.

LEFT *This Hupa female shaman wears a headband and dentalium necklace and holds two small baskets in a photograph by Edward Curtis, part of his study of Athapascan cultures of the northwest. Dentalium was a prized shell to the Hupa, considered a reward from the Immortals, and used as currency and in important ceremonies such as the "World Renewal" ceremonies.*

BELOW *This hunting basket was passed between the Yokuts, who lived west of the Sierra Mountains in California's central valley and foothills, and the Mono Band, who lived east of the range. It signaled the beginning of the hunting season in which the two tribes cooperated.*

# Native Americans and the Civil War

**T**he role of Native Americans in the Civil War is more than just an historical footnote. Organized groups of warriors, allied to either the Union or Confederacy, took part in battles, joined the forces of the North or South individually, acted as scouts, or formed Indian Home Guard units. The Five Civilized Tribes of the Indian Territory, feeling antipathy toward the government that removed them from their land, and with economic and cultural ties to the states of the South, contributed the greatest support for the Confederacy among Native American tribes. The first large-scale test of Native American fighters came as warriors of these tribes joined Texas volunteers to oppose a federal force at Pea Ridge, Arkansas, on March 7–8, 1862.

**ABOVE** *The Battle of Pea Ridge, fought March 7–8, 1862 was the first major Civil War engagement in which Native American forces fought for the South. Mounted Cherokees made up a portion of Major General Earl Van Dorn's command, but the well-positioned Federal forces with their line of artillery quickly scattered the Indians and drove them from the field on March 8. This fanciful period lithograph incorrectly portrayed the Cherokee fighters in war bonnets.*

A number of Indian revolts took place during the Civil War. The Dakota—then known as the Santee Sioux, and Minnesota's main tribe—had sold most of their land to the federal government in 1851, and were moved to a reservation along the Minnesota River. But as the Civil War progressed, white immigration into the state continued to increase. In August 1862, under Chief Little Crow, they attacked settlers in the vicinity of the Lower Sioux Agency, killing 800 during the uprising, taking prisoners, destroying property, and driving the survivors into Fort Ridgely. On August 18, they attacked the agency and assaulted Fort Ridgely on August 20 and 22, but the garrison there held. The Sioux attacked the German settlement of New Ulm on August 19 and 25, but were driven off by the settlers there. On September 2, at Birch Coulee, Sioux warriors surprised a camp of Minnesota volunteers and pinned them down for 36 hours until relief arrived.

Alarmed at these developments, the Governor of Minnesota commissioned Henry Hastings Sibley as colonel and put him in charge of newly-enlisted Minnesota volunteers. On September 19, Sibley's expedition of 1,400 set out from Fort Ridgely to put down the uprising. On September 23, at Wood Lake, near the Upper Sioux Agency, the Minnesota soldiers dealt Little Crow a serious defeat, capturing 2,000 and scattering the rest. Little Crow fled with a number of his followers to Dakota Territory. In total, 307 captured warriors were tried and found responsible for the uprising. President Lincoln pardoned all but 38 who were hanged in Mankato on December 26, 1862, in the largest public execution in U.S. history.

In the summer of 1863, as the Dakota Territory was being settled, Major General John Pope launched a two-pronged offensive against the Dakota before they could harass homesteaders. In July, Sibley led a force against the

**BELOW** *The Santee Sioux (Dakota) under Little Crow terrorized settlements in western Minnesota during the 1862 uprising. Here a group of frightened women and children, led by armed men, pause to rest in their flight from the area.*

**LEFT** *Fort Snelling, Minnesota, at the confluence of the Mississippi and Minnesota Rivers, was a strategic trading center and military outpost before the Civil War. During the war it served as regional headquarters for Major General John Pope and other U.S. Army officials, and as a prison camp for captured warriors.*

**BELOW** *Though reluctant at first, Chief Little Crow led the Dakota on raids against white settlers in the Minnesota River Valley and then clashed with soldiers until defeated at Wood Lake. He fled to Dakota but returned to Minnesota with a few companions in 1863 and was killed by two farmers.*

## ELY PARKER

Ely S. Parker was an educated Seneca who was practicing law in Galena, Illinois, at the outbreak of the Civil War. There he met Ulysses S. Grant. When Grant became commander of the Division of Southern Illinois and Eastern Missouri, he invited Parker to join his headquarters staff. Parker rose to the rank of colonel and wrote out the terms of the Confederate surrender at Appomattox. When Grant became president in 1869, he appointed Parker Commissioner of Indian Affairs, the first Native American in the post. But Parker was a victim of the political corruption scandals that wracked the Grant administration and he was forced to resign the post. He died in poverty in 1895.

Dakota, who had joined forces with their Nakota and Lakota brethren. On July 24, Sibley advanced on a "big mound" rising from among the ravines, and with artillery support scattered the warriors. After the Battle of Big Mound, Sibley pursued the Dakota and broke the force in two more actions, at Dead Buffalo Lake on July 26 and Stone Lake on July 28.

The other prong of Pope's offensive was a force under Brigadier General Alfred Sully. On September 3, 1863 at Whitestone Hill, Sully's men routed the Indians from their camp. Sully's force of 2,500 then advanced and established Fort Rice at the mouth of the Cannonball River on July 7, 1864. Pope sent infantry to back up Sully and the army built more forts. The cavalry continued west and found a large camp on the Little Missouri River. After a conference with tribal leaders failed, Sully attacked the camp at Killdeer Mountain on July 28 and the warriors gave ground. The Battle of Killdeer Mountain broke the back of the Sioux resistance and allowed a new military presence that kept the area relatively peaceful until the end of the Civil War.

Indian Territory saw battles between the North and South during the middle years of the war. Former Indian agents who gained general commissions encouraged Cherokees and others to join the Confederacy. But Native Americans loyal to the Union formed units in Kansas and Missouri under white officers, and marched south to oppose these Rebels. At Chustenahlah (1861,) Old Fort Wayne (1862,) and Honey Springs (1863,) as well as other places in Indian Territory and the Trans-Mississippi region, the Confederates scored a few victories, but ultimately the Rebel forces were contained, then destroyed by the Federals.

The Chiricahua Apache role in the war against the United States began in 1861 when a well-known chief, Cochise, was falsely accused of a raid and the incident led to bloodshed. Then in a skirmish at Apache Pass, Arizona, he escaped U.S. soldiers under Lieutenant George Bascom. From that point, Cochise and his band harassed the whites in the area, including Brigadier General Carlton's California column, which was marching from Tucson to New Mexico to aid in the fight against Confederate soldiers there. After several patrols were ambushed, Carlton sent a force that on July 15–16, 1862 managed to dislodge the Apaches under Cochise and Mangas Colorado. Carlton then ordered a detachment to build Fort Bowie at Apache Pass.

In another sad chapter in American history, Colonel John Chivington, who had a successful Civil War record previously, inflicted a major injustice on peaceful Native Americans in Colorado. Backed by the governor of that state, Chivington massacred several hundred Cheyenne and Arapaho under Chief Black Kettle at Sand Creek, Colorado in November 1864. Another unjustified massacre of Native Americans had occurred at Bear Creek in Idaho the previous year.

In November 1864, General Carlton formed an expedition of more than 800 soldiers and Indian allies under Christopher "Kit" Carson, to move against warriors attacking whites on the Santa Fe Trail. After a few weeks on the march in the Texas panhandle, the force came upon a village of about 1,000 Kiowa which Carson attacked at dawn on November 25. But as the soldiers continued their advance toward an old trading post known as Adobe Walls, they were met by a number of Kiowa and Comanche braves that equaled their own. Carson was able to extricate his force under artillery fire and on the withdrawal back to New Mexico he destroyed the Kiowa village.

**LEFT** *Douglas Cooper was a U.S. Indian agent who gained the trust of Cherokees and others who sympathized with the rebellious South in the Civil War. He was appointed commander of the Confederate Indian Department and was later promoted from colonel to brigadier general. Cooper battled against Chief Opothleyahola and his Creeks and Seminoles in 1861–62, but his army was dealt its serious blow by a superior Union force in the Battle of Honey Springs on July 17, 1863.*

**ABOVE** *President Abraham Lincoln is shown receiving Comanche leaders at the Executive Mansion, as the White House was called then, in this period hand-colored etching. Though Lincoln spent most of his presidency focused on winning the Civil War, he still had many other duties, including working for a reduction of friction between Native Americans and settlers in the Great Plains region.*

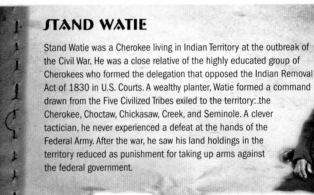

## STAND WATIE

Stand Watie was a Cherokee living in Indian Territory at the outbreak of the Civil War. He was a close relative of the highly educated group of Cherokees who formed the delegation that opposed the Indian Removal Act of 1830 in U.S. Courts. A wealthy planter, Watie formed a command drawn from the Five Civilized Tribes exiled to the territory: the Cherokee, Choctaw, Chickasaw, Creek, and Seminole. A clever tactician, he never experienced a defeat at the hands of the Federal Army. After the war, he saw his land holdings in the territory reduced as punishment for taking up arms against the federal government.

**LEFT** *Chief Black Kettle was the most conciliatory to whites of all Cheyenne leaders in the mid-nineteenth century. He even led a peace delegation t in 1864. The answer he received was the destruction of his village at Sand Creek.*

**BACKGROUND** *The Sand Creek Massacre was one of the most tragic stories of the Civil War. Chief Black Kettle had brought his Cheyenne village to a camp designated by the Bureau of Indian Affairs but the Governor of Colorado ordered action against it. On November 29, 1864, the village was indiscriminately wiped out.*

**Documents**

ITEM 10. This document in President Lincoln's own hand lists the names of 25 Dakota warriors who were held in custody after the Sioux uprising of 1862, but were given presidential pardon in 1864. They and others escaped the mass hanging at Mankato in December 1862.

ITEM 11. Chief Black Kettle composed this "peace letter" and personally delivered it to the Colorado Territorial Governor, Joseph Brown, in Denver. It did not quell the governor's ambition to rid the territory of Native Americans to attract more white settlement. Black Kettle vainly waived the document in the air during the Sand Creek Massacre.

**(See pocket page 43.)**

# Farmers, Ranchers, and Native Americans

By the 1860s, the United States had completed the acquisition, by treaty, purchase or conquest, of the territory that would eventually make up the 48 contiguous states. The end of the Civil War in 1865 had reunited the country and the dream of Manifest Destiny—the building of a continuous nation from Atlantic to Pacific—was once again achievable. But that was for the white nation. What about the Indian nation? For the Native Americans, it was a land of shrinking territory and resources. Those tribes that had been pushed west of the Mississippi River now found that white settlers were competing with them for the resources on which they depended. Their hold on viable hunting and farming land was reduced to just those areas where reservations were created or land set aside for them by an ever changing inventory of treaties.

## CEREMONIAL DANCES OF THE PLAINS TRIBES

Plains Indians held many kinds of rituals. Sun dances are among the most famous. This is a generic term for a variety of ceremonies in which tribal members come together each year during summertime. Their goals were to celebrate the renewal of the universe, which involved fasting and sacrifice, and to seek health and prosperity for their community. The painting above shows another of these ceremonies, the Mandan Buffalo Dance. A more recent ritual adopted by the plains tribes, with significant impact, was the Ghost Dance.

*LEFT A sketch of Native American gumbo sellers at New Orleans French Market. Members of the Opelousas, Coushatta, Chitimacha, Bayougoula, and other tribes eluded efforts by the expanding white population to push them onto reservations and faded into the bayous. They would bring food products from their catches and harvests to the city to sell and support themselves.*

The Indians of the Great Plains considered the vast area between the Mississippi and Rocky Mountains as their open hunting ground and they challenged the white settlements in new ways. They tolerated the initial incursions of the whites who passed through the prairie on the way to somewhere else, stopping only briefly at trading posts and forts, even though these Anglo-European travelers brought with them diseases that devastated Native American tribes who became exposed to them. But by the middle of the nineteenth century, the whites were passing through in increasing numbers, bringing with them livestock that consumed the prairie grass, and wagons that created rutted trails that disrupted the migrations of the bison. Even worse, many of these settlers were stopping on the plains, carving out homes and farms from the new states and territories being formed there. Soon towns began to dot the landscape, and railroad and telegraph lines began to connect the towns.

Nowhere was this scenario more evident than in Texas. Formerly a Mexican possession and then an independent state, its vast expanse represented a varied climate and topography. From the lowlands of the east and the central hills, to the buttes and high desert plateaus of the west, Texas attracted settlements, farms, and even plantations in the southeastern part of the state. But the greatest impact on the Indians was from the large cattle ranches stretching across hundred of acres of central and west Texas. The Comanches and the Kiowa, along with another tribe that adopted the plains lifestyle, the Kiowa Apaches, had come down from the mountains in pre-contact times and developed into skilled bison hunters. The Comanches and Kiowas were dominant in the southern plains, just as the Lakota and Cheyenne were to the north.

It became obvious to these tribes in Texas and elsewhere in the plains that they needed to retaliate against the impact on their hunting by the white settlers. Cattle rustling and raids became prevalent. The ranchers were already locked in a struggle with farmers—whom they termed "sod busters"—who were cutting into their grazing land. The disturbances caused by the Indians aggravated an already tense situation. Law enforcement agencies, vigilante groups, and soldiers went after Indian war parties and settlements.

*BELOW LEFT This photograph, from the Matthew Brady collection, shows a large delegation of Native American chiefs and government officials outside the White House in the mid-1800s. Although these meetings were designed to promote goodwill, the course of federal policy toward disposing of more Indian land to settlers was not changing.*

*RIGHT Charles Russell, one of the noted early artists to chronicle Native Americans, drew this sketch of an Indian village moving in 1905. The nomadic tribes of the plains followed the bison migrations, however by the early twentieth century, free-roaming bison herds were in deep decline and most of the tribes of the Great Plains had been forced onto reservations.*

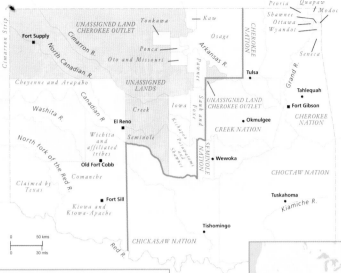

ABOVE *A settler painted this scene of the May 9, 1847 peace council at Fredericksburg, Texas during which the Meusebach Treaty was signed by the German Immigrant Company representative, John Meusebach, and war chiefs of the Comanche and Delaware tribes. The treaty was considered fair at the time, but the inevitable expansion of settlers to the Lone Star state destroyed Comanche hunting grounds.*

RIGHT *Wovoka was a Paiute living and working as a ranch hand in western Nevada. He adopted white clothing and ways and was known in the community as Jack Wilson. During a vision, as he described it, he visited heaven and God brought forth the spirits of dead ancestors and taught him that Indians who lived in peace and goodness would join their ancestors in a new world on earth. The main feature of Wovoka's mix of traditional spiritualism and Christian faith was the Ghost Dance.*

RIGHT *After the Civil War, this group of Cherokee leaders went to Washington to appeal the case of their people in the face of the planned U.S. policy to carve other reservations out of their land to punish those Cherokees who fought for the Confederacy. Among those pictured are John Rollins Ridge, son of John Ridge (left,) Saladin Watie, son of Stand Watie (second from left,) and Elias Cornelius Boudinot, son of Elias Boudinot (second from right.)*

The isolated incidents of raids and massacres on both sides escalated into a full-scale frontier war. For example, in 1835, a special militia, the Texas Rangers, was formed to fight Indians while the Texas regulars were battling the Mexican Army. Besides traditional weapons and tactics, the Indians used firearms (traded or stolen) to augment their warring capabilities. Liquor enhanced or supplanted traditional spiritual ideals of invincibility. But the firepower and organization of the forces ranged against them were too great to allow the Native Americans more than transitory victories. The frontier war would continue with tragic results for the white, but more especially for the Native American populations, for the remainder of the century.

## MANHOOD RITUALS

Native American men in virtually every tribe prove their manhood in hunting and warfare. But individual tribes have other traditions. Many cultures use sweat-houses in which men spend time for spiritual enlightenment, camaraderie, and cleansing. The transition to manhood during puberty is treated in some cultures by isolating and/or drugging the boy in an attempt to induce visions, or subjecting him to the tests and tutelage of elders. The most grotesque manhood rituals are those used by the Plains tribes that involve bodily mutilation. The most common of these is the suspension of the body by skewers through the breast as part of the Sun Dance.

**Indian Territory in 1888**

- • Towns
- ▪ Forts
- Unassigned lands
- —— Boundary between land retained and land relinquished by the Five Civilized Tribes after the Civil War

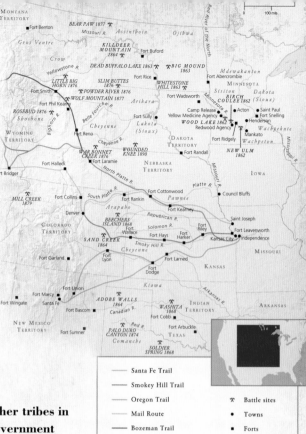

**LEFT** *General William T. Sherman (third from left facing the camera,) general-in-chief of the U.S. Army, and other peace commissioners meet in May 1868 with Lakota, Cheyenne, and other chiefs of the northern plains to negotiate an end to hostilities in the region. The result of the meeting was the second Treaty of Fort Laramie.*

**BELOW** *This Henry repeating rifle was presented to the Oglala Sioux chief Sitting Bull the Minor (or the Good) by President Ulysses S. Grant on June 6, 1875. Sitting Bull the Minor was one of the Lakota chiefs who adhered to the terms of the Treaty of Fort Laramie. However he was killed by rival Crow warriors during a hunting expedition on the Tongue River on December 16, 1876.*

Notable forts, trails, and "Indian War" battles on the Great Plains.

# Last of the Great Warriors— Dakota and Other Plains Tribes

Scattered raids by the Dakota, Nakota, Lakota, Cheyenne, and other tribes in Colorado, Kansas, and Wyoming Territory caused the federal government to focus more attention on the frontier problem in the period following the Civil War. Prominent veteran officers who remained in the U.S. Army were at the forefront of the military response to Native American raids and attacks. Attacks on settlers led to a retaliatory campaign by Civil War hero Winfield Scott Hancock on the Cheyenne of Kansas and Colorado in 1867. Seeing a robust force of warriors still present among the Teton Sioux (Lakota,) who were made up of the Oglala Sioux and other groups, the administration of President Ulysses S. Grant sent the army's top soldier, William T. Sherman, and others in a peace commission to meet with Chief Red Cloud of the Oglala Sioux.

*BOTTOM LEFT Curly (Ashishishe,) pictured here in later life, was a young Crow who scouted for Custer in the expedition that led the golden-haired commander to his final battle at Little Bighorn. Mortal enemies of the Lakota, the Crow willingly scouted for the U.S. Army. Finally seeing the danger to his force, Custer released his Crow scouts and Curly survived the massacre.*

*LEFT This headdress belonging to Crazy Horse was made of the skin and feathers of the red-backed hawk. In addition, he wore into battle a lightning bolt painted across his face and dots representing hail, images that came to him in a vision quest he experienced at an early age.*

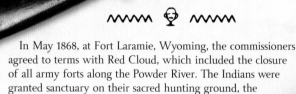

In May 1868, at Fort Laramie, Wyoming, the commissioners agreed to terms with Red Cloud, which included the closure of all army forts along the Powder River. The Indians were granted sanctuary on their sacred hunting ground, the Black Hills, as long as they maintained peace and abided by the treaty. Relative calm came to the area, and the Bozeman Trail through Montana, for six years.

Then word circulated of an important gold find in South Dakota's Black Hills. Miners came to the area, guarded by an army expedition under George Armstrong Custer. The treaty was violated and a new wave of violence commenced in 1876. Custer and other cavalry commanders, under the overall command of Brigadier General Alfred Terry, battled the Indians in Montana and the Dakotas to force them onto reservations. On June 17, the Lakota scored a major victory over Brigadier General George Crook's forces at the Battle of the Rosebud in Montana Territory. Terry ordered Custer

## SITTING BULL

Sitting Bull was a Hunkpapa medicine man who led the Lakota in the latter part of the nineteenth century. He is best known for defeating George Armstrong Custer at the Battle of Little Bighorn in 1876. After the U.S. Army regained control of the area, Sitting Bull fled to Canada with some of his followers. He returned in 1881 and was placed on a reservation, becoming something of a celebrity and even participating in Buffalo Bill Cody's Wild West Show. When the Lakota embraced violence during the Ghost Dance movement, Sitting Bull was killed by Indian police while resisting arrest on December 15, 1890.

*"They made many promises and only kept one, they promised to take our land and they did"*

**Chief Red Cloud**

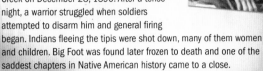

## BIG FOOT

Big Foot was a Lakota chief who was firmly dedicated to the Ghost Dance belief. Shaken by the fate that befell Sitting Bull at Standing Rock, he and his followers fled their homes near the Cheyenne River Agency and headed for the Black Hills. The 7th Cavalry surrounded their camp at Wounded Knee Creek on December 28, 1890. After a tense night, a warrior struggled when soldiers attempted to disarm him and general firing began. Indians fleeing the tipis were shot down, many of them women and children. Big Foot was found later frozen to death and one of the saddest chapters in Native American history came to a close.

to advance on the Sioux, but to avoid an immediate engagement. Convinced he would be successful in routing an encampment of Oglala Sioux, Cheyenne, and Arapaho under spiritual leader Sitting Bull, Custer took his 7th Cavalry to the Little Bighorn River on June 25, 1876.

There he divided his command into three segments. While Custer's two subordinates failed to gain any advantage, Custer took 210 men toward the camp from the east. At the Little Bighorn, warriors under Crazy Horse massacred Custer and his men, scalping them and leaving no soldiers to survive. The rest of the 7th was pinned down for two days until the Indians broke camp as Terry approached. The war continued for nearly a year. Crazy Horse surrendered in 1877, but was killed by a guard. By the end of the decade, the surviving Native Americans of the Great Plains had been forced onto smaller reservations. Sitting Bull fled to Canada with some of his people in 1876, then returned four years later and was placed on a reservation.

About this time, a new spiritual phenomenon swept through the Indians on the reservations. The Ghost Dance was a religious philosophy that told of Native Americans being reunited with their dead ancestors, and the return of the earth to the favorable conditions of an earlier time. By 1890, the Teton Dakota had begun disturbances on the reservations, bringing a violent reaction from the white authorities to the spread of the Ghost Dance. Sitting Bull was killed while resisting arrest at Standing Rock Agency in North Dakota during a disturbance associated with the Ghost Dance. After Sitting Bull was killed, Big Foot took control of the Lakota. In December 1890, the army under Major General Nelson A. Miles defeated (many say massacred) Big Foot's band at Wounded Knee Creek in South Dakota, virtually ending resistance by the warriors of the Great Plains tribes.

**TOP LEFT** *A photo of Lieutenant Colonel George A. Custer's 7th Cavalry. The unit was based at Fort Abraham Lincoln near Bismarck, North Dakota, and the troopers' first assignment was to guard work parties surveying for the Northern Pacific Railroad. Later, Custer led the unit into the Black Hills of South Dakota with prospectors seeking gold. Custer constantly underestimated the ability of Native American warriors to stand and fight for land and family.*

**ABOVE** *This nineteenth-century color lithograph of the June 25, 1876 Battle of Little Big Horn dramatizes the greatest victory of the Plains Indians over the U.S. Army. The topography was quite different. The five companies of the 7th Cavalry led by Custer were on a plateau east of the river and the allied warriors charged up from the river. There were no tall mountains in the immediate area. Custer was dressed in buckskin that day with his hair cut short.*

**BELOW** *A Ghost Dance ceremony on an unidentified reservation. The ceremonies were intensely personal to the participants and photographers had to take pictures without being noticed by the dancers.*

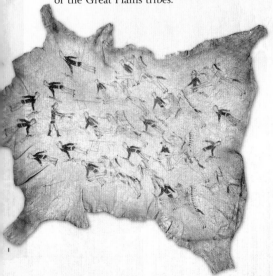

**LEFT** *Cheyenne artist Lame Deer illustrated the attack at Little Bighorn on dismounted cavalry troopers by mounted Lakota and Cheyenne warriors on deer hide to commemorate the greatest Native American victory in the western Indian wars.*

# Last of the Great Warriors—Apache and Comanche Tribes

**T**he Comanches, Kiowas and Kiowa Apaches saw their dominance of the Texas plains come to an end during the second half of the nineteenth century, but the struggle raged until 1875. While other tribes of the plains were making peace or war to the north, these warriors continued their raiding on Texas ranchers and settlers, although with decreasing success. Texas Rangers (the state mounted police force) and Indian fighters drove the Comanche and Kiowa raiders into the panhandle region. The war parties then turned their attention to settlers, stages, and supply trains using the Santa Fe Trail through northern New Mexico.

**ABOVE** *Chiricahua Apache prisoners, including in the first row Chief Naiche, center, and Geronimo, second from right, were photographed in a stop during their rail transfer from Fort Bowie, Arizona to confinement at Fort Marion, St. Augustine, Florida. Geronimo, Naiche, and another chief, Chihuahua, surrendered their bands to the U.S. Army on September 4, 1886.*

Northwest Texas and northeastern New Mexico were still subject to Indian raids after the Civil War. The government first tried to negotiate peace treaties. In August 1865, a meeting was arranged to bring together tribes of the region and government negotiators, including Kit Carson, to offer reservation land and limited hunting off the reservations in exchange for peace. The resulting Little Arkansas Treaty was signed on October 14, but the state governments of Texas and Kansas, as well as a society of Cheyenne warriors known as the "Dog Soldiers" refused to recognize the accord. Fighting and raids broke out again in the north. Again, the government tried to negotiate, offering land in Indian Territory taken from those tribes that had sided with the Confederacy. The Treaty of Medicine Lodge in 1867 brought together many tribes, but some warriors continued raiding, even as other chiefs led groups of their followers toward the new reservations.

Major General Philip Sheridan formed three columns to converge on the recalcitrant tribes and drive them onto the reservations. Overcoming resistance from the warriors as he went, by 1869 Sheridan had got most of the southern plains Indians onto reservations. There were some tragedies along the way, such as George Custer's senseless massacre of Cheyennes at Washita in November 1868. But renegade bands led by the Quahada Comanches—who signed no treaties—continued to attack whites. A new Kiowa leader, Satanta, emerged to join them. He led warriors on raids against the Texans even while living on the reservation. In May 1871, he was arrested in a confrontation with General W.T. Sherman at Fort Sill, was tried and imprisoned.

The Quahada, under their chief Quanah Parker, remained on the rampage for another four years, fighting white hunters who competed with them for the shrinking bison herds. After Indian fighters resisted an attack by Quanah's warriors near Adobe Walls in 1874, 5,000 Kiowa, Cheyenne, and Comanche people fled the

**LEFT** *This photograph is of "Naches" or "Wei-chi-ti" (Naiche,) the Chiricahua Apache chief who was the son of Cochise. He is pictured with his wife and is holding a rifle. He was imprisoned for a time at Fort Marion with Geronimo and other Apache leaders.*

**LEFT** *Quanah Parker was a Quahada Comanche war chief, the son of a white mother kidnapped by the tribe as a girl and a Comanche chieftain. With Quahada war parties, he raided and warred against the army, who respected his leadership. When he finally surrendered, he was a tireless protector of the rights of his people on the reservation, prospered in trade, and supported the Peyote Cult.*

## COCHISE

Cochise was the leader of the Chokonen Band of Chiricahua Apaches. Like Mangas Colorado and other Apache leaders of the mid-1800s, he led his bands on raids into Mexico, his people's foe over many generations. He did not attack the Americans moving through and into the area around Apache Pass, until the Bascom Affair, in which Cochise was arrested when he went to parlay with an army officer over an allegation of kidnap against the Chiricahua. From then on the waged war against the soldiers—including during the Battle of Apache Pass in 1862—until in 1871 he was forced onto the Chiricahua Reservation where, three years later, he died.

# GERONIMO

Goyahkla, "one who yawns," grew up in a peaceful mountainside community of Chiricahua Apaches. After achieving warrior status, Goyahkla alternately raided and traded with the Mexicans. In 1850, Mexican soldiers raided his camp while he was away, killing his mother, wife, and his three babies. He led a retaliatory raid against them, and from the ferocity of his reaction was thereafter known as Geronimo, derived from the plea for mercy to St. Jerome uttered by his victims. His bravery and tactical skill brought him to the attention of Cochise and Mangas Colorado, whom he fought under. After their deaths, he assumed leadership of the Chiricahua until he and his band were cornered in 1886. Exiled to Fort Marion in Florida, he was then brought to Fort Sill, Oklahoma, where he dictated his memoirs while under house arrest.

reservation, fearing retaliation. They followed the Red River west, taking refuge in the deep canyons of the area. However the U.S. Cavalry pursued them, and in late September, they were dealt a serious blow when troopers under Colonel Ranald Mackenzie discovered and destroyed a large camp at Palo Duro Canyon. The last of the surviving refugees were forced back onto the reservation by the spring of 1875, and individual leaders were banished to a Florida military prison to maintain the peace.

Farther west, another group of Apaches, the Chiricahua, attacked troops and travelers on the roads west, using their homes in the mountains on what is now the Arizona-New Mexico border as a base, and exploiting increased mobility from stolen horses. When the United States acquired the region from Mexico, the Apaches initially made peace with the newcomers. Trouble began when the Americans, bound by treaty, policed Apache raids south into Mexico. During the Civil War, Cochise was detained when the Chiricahua were accused of kidnapping a rancher's son and his confrontation with Lieutenant George Bascom escalated into bad blood between the army and the Apaches Cochise and the Chiricahuas finally submitted to settlement on a reservation southeast of Fort Bowie.

But after the old warrior died, young Apaches tired of reservation life and resumed marauding and killing. Then, in 1876, the government moved them to the more inhospitable San Carlos Reservation in the desert to the west. The unrest grew. From these events emerged Geronimo, the greatest warrior of the southwest, to lead the Chiricahua. Even though he was not a chief, his exemplary courage and fighting spirit inspired many Apaches to wage ferocious raids on the settlers and soldiers of southeastern Arizona. Geronimo took a group of warriors and left the reservation for Mexico. First General George Crook, who had great respect for the Apache fighting ability and spirit, tried to bring Geronimo and his bands to terms in May 1885. But the Chiricahua continued to resist until General Nelson Miles, who had brought about the surrender of several tribes on the northern plains, maneuvered Geronimo into a position where he was forced in September 1886 to surrender, bringing a close to the Native American violence in the southwest.

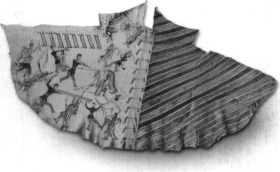

**LEFT** *This tipi hide cover containing battle pictures is also called Do-Gíägyä-Gúät in Native language. It probably depicts Kiowa or Comanche warriors battling U.S. Army cavalry and infantry. It was included in a comprehensive 1898 report from the Bureau of American Ethnology, Smithsonian Institution.*

**TOP LEFT** *This rawhide shield with a design of double-ended hooks in blue paint was picked up by an American soldier who fought in the Mexican War. Along with the shield, which has a wooden handle on the back held by leather thongs, is a "potato masher" carved wooden war club. The weapons are believed to be Pima in origin and the design could be Hopi, or influenced by Spanish Basque settlers.*

**BACKGROUND** *Two men pose with rifles on an Apache rancheria. After the reservation proved not to be satisfactory for teaching the Chiricahuas to increase their use of agriculture in the arid southwest, the government set up smaller rancherias, communal farms where the residents grew hay and other crops for sale and trade.*

**FAR LEFT** *The woodcut illustration on this* Harper's Weekly *cover from April 24, 1886 brought the Apache War into the homes of America. The bottom lithograph is from a photograph of a meeting between General George Crook and Geronimo and other holdout Chiricahua leaders.*

# Alaskan and Arctic Tribes Meet the Age of Industrialization

As the twentieth century began, those Native Americans living at the top of the world preserved a culture that had in many ways remained unchanged for thousands of years. Large-scale contact with whites had been taking place for nearly 150 years, as Russian and British traders established outposts on the coastal and island areas, and then began to establish communities. A greater impact on the Eskimo population occurred through the introduction of their manufactured goods, culture, and religions. But the natives continued to live their lives much as their ancestors had done.

In 1867, the United States purchased Alaska from Russia. Meanwhile, the newly constituted Dominion of Canada, which had achieved increased autonomy from Great Britain, established its own policies and methods for dealing with the natives. Certain segments of the Eskimo and sub-Arctic Eyak populations began to feel a greater impact from the white influx. Besides the trading communities that grew from the initial outposts, the whites set up whaling and fishing operations with bases in the coastal areas. Then the discovery of gold deposits in Alaska and Canada along the Yukon River in 1897 led to an inrush of prospectors and consequently huge impact on the Native Americans, as the newcomers and their camps encroached on the traditional hunting grounds of the inland sub-arctic groups. By the 1920s, however, the gold deposits were tapped out, and any incidental benefits accrued by the native population ended.

By this time, the Eyak tribe still roamed vast areas of the sub-arctic, continuing their traditions of hunting, gathering, and occasional cultivation, although they were being nudged aside in some areas by Blackfeet and Blood Indians, who had been driven north from their own traditional hunting grounds, and by the white prospectors. The Eskimos, categorized in the twentieth century into three general groups, the Aleuts, Yupik, and Inuit (Eskimo for "people,") found themselves in competition with the new technology of white entrepreneurs for the sea mammals and fish that provided the food and materials for their survival. Even so, the last group of isolated tribesmen of the Arctic Sea, the Copper Eskimos, had never seen a European before 1910.

**TOP** *This photograph shows Eskimos harpooning a whale at Point Barrow, Alaska. The animal is at or near expiration so the ceremony of thanksgiving, a time-honored tradition of connection between the spirit of the people and the spirit of the animal, is set to begin.*

**ABOVE LEFT** *The Miles Brothers photographed two Tlingit women and several children along the Kotsina River, Alaska in 1902.*

## JAPANESE OCCUPATION IN THE ALEUTIAN ISLANDS

During World War II, the Japanese seized the western portion of the Aleutian Islands. Parishes of the Russian Orthodox Church, like this one in the village of Attu, ministered to the spiritual needs of the Aleut villagers during the Japanese occupation and military rule. The presence of the church and the priests gave a sense of stability to the people in a time when, for a period of four years, their world was turned upside down.

**BELOW** *Early twentieth-century Eskimo goggles. Like their ancestors centuries earlier, Inuit of the early twentieth century survived by hunting caribou and other mammals on the tundra and frozen shoreline as well as depending on sea mammals and fish. These goggles helped the Eskimos prevent snow blindness on hunting excursions.*

Gradually, many of the Eskimos and the Eyak adopted the products of modernization, while still holding onto many of their traditional methods and customs. Woolen clothing, rifles, and sail-power entered their lives. While firearms and liquor were officially banned by the governments of the U.S., Canada, and Denmark (which ruled Greenland,) they were traded nevertheless, with often devastating and deadly consequences for the native populations. Some natives found work in the mining camps, canneries, steam whaling fleets, and later military installations, of the whites. Others had to compete with them, but found value in the trade of baleen (whalebone) and blubber, until newer technology cut the demand for those products. In the 1920s fox fur was in vogue, but the Great Depression cut the demand. These market fluctuations created a great deal of economic stress for those Native Americans who depended on trade rather than traditional hunting and fishing for survival.

Shortly before World War II, the governments of the U.S. and Canada began to formulate national policies for their northern native populations, a development the Danish government had undertaken years earlier in Greenland. Schools and medical facilities followed in the wake of those the missionaries had established long before. But with government organization and aid came regulation, especially laws regarding wildlife exploitation and land conservation. For the Native Americans of the north, these ideas were foreign to their cultural traditions which allowed the taking only of what they needed and the caring for the spirits of their animal prey. Gradually, the blend of old and new meshed, but the discovery of oil in 1968 along Alaska's Prudhoe Bay brought a new round of struggles between the original inhabitants and the governments who sought to impose their own rules.

**ABOVE** *Ola, a beautiful Noatak woman, poses with her husband and child. The expressive faces of the Arctic people relay the natural goodness and joy of life that emanates from deep inside them.*

**RIGHT** *Simiguluk, an Eskimo spear and lance maker at Point Barrow, Alaska, proudly displays some of his handiwork to photographer Stanley Morgan in 1935.*

**BELOW RIGHT** *Knik Chief Nikaly and his family are pictured in a 1910 photograph taken near Anchorage, Alaska by H.G. Kaiser.*

**BOTTOM** *This 1927 photograph shows a group of Inupiat kayakers at Noatak, Alaska. Their double-ended paddles are shown at the ready on calm waters, but the Eskimos can dig them into the brine at a moment's notice, turning on the spot and swiftly pursuing prey.*

## THE MODERN ARCTIC HUNTER

Hunting and fishing still play important roles in the lives of many Eskimos. Seals, whales, polar bears, fish, game birds, and other animals are still pursued, whether for commercial sale or personal consumption. The modern hunter often uses technology to his advantage. Snowmobiles, fiberglass kayaks, motorized canoes, harpoon guns, and winches have often replaced traditional man- and dog-power, animal-skin disguises, weapons with wooden shafts, and sealskin boats. However some hunters still occasionally use age-tested tools and methods. Eskimos still take part in traditional ceremonies to bring bountiful harvests, engage in competitions to keep their bodies in shape, and perform rituals to release the souls of their prey.

# Allotment and Reform— Native Americans Enter the Twentieth Century

T he last part of the nineteenth century saw a major shift in the way the United States government viewed the Native American population. This change came about as a result of the Dawes Act, a piece of legislation sponsored by Senator Henry Dawes of Massachusetts and passed by Congress on February 8, 1887. Proponents argued that Native Americans should have an opportunity to own farm land individually, just as white Americans had. They argued that many Native Americans were taking on the ways of whites, and should therefore be treated equally. The land was taken from breaking up the old reservations into sections. Each head of household would receive 120 acres, with half that amount doled out to single persons and orphans, and 30 acres to non-orphans under 18 years of age.

**TOP** *Coach Glenn Warner (standing back row, center) is pictured with the 1912 track and field team of the Carlisle Indian School. Warner accompanied two members of the team, Jim Thorpe and Hopi long-distance runner Louis Tewanima, as their coach to the 1912 Olympics in Stockholm, Sweden.*

**ABOVE** *A Potawatomie woman weaves outside a reservation dwelling.*

**BELOW** *Chief Yellow Bear poses with his daughter at the Carlisle Indian Industrial School at the turn of the century. The school was founded in 1879 by former U.S. Army officer Richard Henry Pratt, who had first practiced his rehabilitation theories on Apache and Arapaho warriors imprisoned at Fort Marion in Florida.*

᠕᠕᠕᠕ 👤 ᠕᠕᠕᠕

**ABOVE** *A Navajo silversmith displays his wares and tools in this 1880 photograph. Turning traditional crafts into a cottage industry appealing to tourists was a major part of tribal adjustment entering the twentieth century.*

**BELOW** *This handbill from May 1879 was designed to attract people to tour land in the Indian Territory. The advertisement claims to offer land not part of any designated reservation. This bill appeared ten years before the Indian and Oklahoma (panhandle region) areas of present-day Oklahoma were opened to homesteading.*

Like most of the federal government's strategies for dealing with the Indians, the Dawes Act had a dual purpose. Besides attempting to modernize the treatment of Indians by treating them as individuals, it was also an attempt to gain more land for—and avoid friction as a result of— the land rushes of the 1890s. This was especially true in Indian Territory, where whites were greedily eyeing Native American tribal reservations. The eventual result was the largest single-day land grab in American history and the formation of the state of Oklahoma. There were exceptions: the reservations of the Five Civilized Tribes and the other long-established tribes of Indian Territory, the Seneca Reservation in New York, and a portion of northwest Nebraska below the Dakota Reservation were exempt from the parceling, at least under the initial law.

The plan was not without its problems and the Bureau of Indian Affairs had a difficult time implementing it. The determination of who was eligible for the land was complicated by the existence of many people of mixed blood. Once the allotments were determined, tribal governments were to be abolished and the Indians were to recognize only federal and state laws. Not only were many Native Americans unfamiliar with individual farming, but a fair number resisted the notion. Of

## Prepare to Meet us AT CHETOPA, KAN.
### A LARGE AREA OF THE BEAUTIFUL
# INDIAN
### TERRITORY OPEN TO HOMESTEADERS.

## FROM INDIAN TERRITORY TO OKLAHOMA

Oklahoma derives its name from the Choctaw words *okla* meaning people and *homa* meaning red. The Indian Territory had been established by the U.S. Congress in the 1830s, but the passage of the Homestead Act in 1862 was a catalyst for an increasing influx of settlers from the 1870s, beginning in the sparsely settled panhandle region. Court decisions paved the way for opening lands to white settlement and the passage of the Dawes Act opened non-tribal lands for survey. President Benjamin Harrison opened two million acres for settlement and the first land run occurred on April 22, 1889. Later settlement was conducted by lottery, and in 1907 the territory became a state.

those who were willing, few had the capital to invest in stock and equipment. Many of the allotments in the west, moreover, were in arid areas unsuitable for farming. There were no clear-cut provisions for passing the land on to heirs, and the allotments of deceased heads of households were divided up into small parcels among their heirs.

Many of those minors who received allotments did so while they were away from their tribes and families attending government boarding schools. Like the schools established earlier by Christian missionaries, the Indian schools were designed to integrate the coming generations of Native Americans into the general population, but without the religious indoctrination of missionary endeavors. The first federal Indian school was established on a military reservation in south central Pennsylvania at Carlisle in 1879. Other schools were established by the federal and state governments around the nation. They did serve the purpose of educating many Native Americans, and raised literacy gave them valuable life skills and prepared some to go on to higher education, sports, and artistic opportunities. But critics argued the students suffered a loss of connection with their tribal roots. In some cases, this was true, in others a mix of Euro-American education was balanced with respect for tradition.

About this time a new non-governmental reform movment was beginning to be heard as well. Seeing the plight of the Indians forced onto increasingly smaller tracts of land, and with government stipends often keeping them in destitution, reformers generated a public outcry for better treatment of America's original habitants. It would be many years before the movement had significant impact. However, as bad as the situation was in the United States, the Dominion of Canada waited another 50 years to implement a central policy to assist their Native American cultures in adapting to the rapid changes that modernization and technology handed them in the twentieth century.

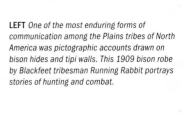

LEFT *One of the most enduring forms of communication among the Plains tribes of North America was pictographic accounts drawn on bison hides and tipi walls. This 1909 bison robe by Blackfeet tribesman Running Rabbit portrays stories of hunting and combat.*

## EDUCATION AND CITIZENSHIP

Cherokee parents in the early nineteenth century encouraged their children to learn English to help them deal with the influx of English-speaking whites. Ever since then, Native American education has gone through fits and starts. The Indian boarding schools, which for a century were at the forefront of assimilation, gave way by the 1950s to schools on reservations. From the Land Allotment Act, Indians were given citizenship when deemed competent to handle their own affairs, increasing the importance of education. The Citizenship Act of 1924 made citizens of all native-born Indians, but with the government still in control of their affairs. Canadian Native Americans were given the status of British subjects in the nineteenth century, but were likewise restricted by government regulation of their affairs.

ABOVE *Indian police remove members of the Cupertino band of Mission Indians from Warner's Ranch in northeast San Diego County to Pala.*

BELOW *This 1872 photograph is of a Chippewa settlement in Canada.*

# The New Deal, Reorganization and Termination

**B**y the 1930s, Canada had caught up with the United States in the process of setting aside land for its Indian tribes, and indeed went on to surpass her southern neighbor in this regard. The United States, having committed 130 million acres of land for Native Americans in 1887 as a result of the Dawes Act, saw that number shrink to 44 million acres by 1933. In the midst of the social reforms spurred by the Great Depression and the election of Franklin D. Roosevelt as U.S. President in 1932, the Bureau of Indian Affairs also gained a new reform-minded director, John Collier. He immediately set about changing government policies toward those Indians on reservations.

Central to his strategy was organizing and empowering the tribal councils on the reservations in their dealing with the government. He engineered congressional passage of the Wheeler-Howard Act on June 18, 1934, which contained a great number of the reforms he envisioned. The act, known as the Indian Reorganization Act when enacted, permitted the tribes to form constitutions and charters and negotiate with the B.I.A. with the force of a united group. Collier took steps to improve food, medical, and growing conditions on the reservations and started an Indian branch of the Civilian Conservation Corps, one of the New Deal work programs. More Native Americans were placed on the B.I.A. payroll and exempted from civil service rules that might have denied them the jobs. Critics of these programs pointed out that not all Native American were ready for the kind of autonomous status the New Deal proponents were willing to dole out, either on an individual or a tribal level.

There was truth in what they said. The former Plains tribes had not adapted well to farming, and continued to survive largely on government rations and annuities. Of the tribes that did adopt constitutions or charters, many simply used the B.I.A. guidelines and failed to incorporate provisions that would gain acceptance among traditionalists in the tribe. For their part, state and local governments did not generally favor the repurchase of lands for the tribes, and many found ways to hold up the federal repurchases on behalf of the Indians. In one of the more controversial but necessary provisions of the act, a "blood quantum system" was established to identify who was a member of a tribe and could therefore qualify for loans and aid. Those who were full or half-blood natives, as well as family members who resided on the reservations at the time the act passed, met the blood quantum test.

One of the positive measures of the New Deal policies was in the formation of rancherias—a Spanish term for the tribal livestock ranches that sprung up in the west. A livestock reduction plan and other conservation measures aimed at raising prices of livestock

## UNITED STATES AND CANADIAN POLICIES

The United States and Canada adopted different emphases in their policies toward their Native American populations. The population of Canadian Indians was less numerous and spread over a wider area. Reservations (reserves) existed in Canada, but did not pose the kind of challenges experienced south of the border. The early recognition of Canadian Indians as British subjects and a non-politicized Indian Bureau gave the appearance that Canada's policy was more fair. But the Canadians had similar problems in settling their Plains tribes and did not welcome refugees from the United States, such as the Dakota and Lakota. Later in the century, policies fell into a kind of lockstep with the U.S., though the Canadians' failed experiment with termination lasted until 1969.

**TOP RIGHT** *An Apache farmer operates a mule-driven plow on the sandy soil of southern Arizona.*

**LEFT** *This photograph is of delegates to a convention of Indian Affairs for all California reservations which took place at Riverside, California in 1930. At the time, the former Mission Indians were struggling to make the desert lands allotted to them into viable reservation communities while the tribes in the northern part of the state were laboring to make their subsistence on rancherias and losing members to urban areas.*

**BOTTOM LEFT** *A photograph of Pop Warner and Blackfeet natives at the 1933 dedication ceremony for the Highway to the Sun, which was built to cross Logan Pass in Glacier National Park from the Blackfeet reservation in Montana. Warner, because he elevated Native American culture as an extremely successful coach and athletic director at Carlisle Indian Industrial School, was greatly revered in the Native American community.*

**BACKGROUND** *Pisehedwin, a Potawatomie Indian, and others gather in front of his Kansas farm home in 1877. Under the Dawes Act individual farming parcels were cut from reservation land. Unlike this tidy farm, most parcels were on lands difficult for even experienced agriculturalists to work.*

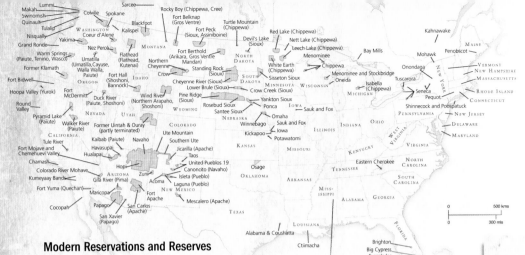

was put in place. In Minnesota, Montana, North and South Dakota, and Arizona particularly, the purchase of additional lands for the tribes went smoothly and credit extension for the purchase of livestock, seed, and equipment opened up great opportunities for tribes in those areas. The value per head of the tribes' stock rose, profits accumulated, and loans were repaid. Programs like 4-H clubs and other youth and family organizations encouraged a sense of cohesion and contributed to the success of the ranches. The New Deal did not cure all the problems that kept many Native Americans in poverty and depression during the time of cultural assimilation, but it was a start.

With the onset of the Second World War, the government moved into a wartime mode. The B.I.A. was transferred to Chicago, employees left or were reassigned, funds were cut, and Japanese-Americans were interned on some reservations. A great number of Native Americans left the reservations to join the armed forces or work in war factories. After Roosevelt's death in 1945, Collier was replaced as the head of the B.I.A. With the post-war economic and population boom, politicians questioned the continued need for federal control of Indian affairs. They now saw assimilation as a realistic goal. More Native Americans were moving to the cities voluntarily or through government-sponsored relocations. Indians and non-Native Americans—for varying motives—lined up on both sides of the argument for "Termination:" the emancipation of all Native Americans from federal stewardship. Though House Resolution 108, passed in 1953, officially began the termination policy, it was carried out in piecemeal.

Two of the initial tribes to experience the effects of termination were the Klamaths of Oregon and the Menominees of Wisconsin. The Klamaths underwent termination, pushed by Indians already living off the reservations, in return for per capita payments laid out in the "Termination" plan. However, many recipients mismanaged their money and the tribe remained in a state of widespread poverty. The Menominee tribe attempted to manage its affairs in the form of a private corporation, but state and local taxation, resource exploitation by outsiders, and a breakdown of services caused the enterprise to fail. Few clear-cut advantages came out of "Termination" and although it dragged into the 1960s, the federal government then turned again to the B.I.A. and new solutions to the problems of the Native American population.

**BELOW LEFT** *Cherokees living in Cherokee North Carolina in 1952. Thanks to the efforts of a white nineteenth-century store clerk named William Holland Thomas, a band of Cherokees who lived in the Great Smoky Mountains of western North Carolina were able to remain on their native lands after removal of the rest of the Cherokee Nation to Indian Territory. Thomas became a lawyer and lobbied for protection of the tribe's rights under an 1819 treaty before the state government of North Carolina and the U.S. Congress.*

## CIVILIAN CONSERVATION CORPS—INDIAN DIVISION

Roosevelt's New Deal policies had their greatest impact in programs aimed to raise the economic status of poorer Americans. Government-created jobs in public works had the dual benefits of an immediate income for the workers and a lasting legacy of improvements to infrastructure. Many Native Americans received opportunities through the C.C.C.–I.D. (Civilian Conservation Corps—Indian Division.) As well as finding work for Native Americans as unskilled laborers on roads, public buildings, and forest conservation, a dedicated effort was made to unleash their artistic talents in creating works of art. These could be producing individual paintings or craft projects in educational settings where the more experienced guided the beginners, or creating paintings, murals, and other works that celebrated Native American heritage.

**ABOVE RIGHT** *Havasupai men proudly display watermelons grown during the 1950 harvest. The Havasupai adapted to farming well on the irrigated lands of northern and western Arizona.*

**RIGHT** *These Seminole men are training to fight forest fires in Florida. Many Native Americans joined the U.S. Forest Service as firefighters in the second part of the twentieth century.*

# Fighting on the Other Side—Native American Soldiers

ative Americans had fought alongside white forces during the French and Indian, Revolutionary, 1812, and Civil Wars. But from the twentieth century, Native Americans no longer fought on the battlefield to retain or regain their land though the fight continued in the courts. Most were living, happily or unhappily, on reservations, or were forced to abandon their culture and integrate with the majority of non-natives in search of work. Opportunities for economic advancement were rare for Indians, most of whom were, at the turn of the century, just beginning to deal with the trauma of assimilation.

**ABOVE** *Three WWII Marine Corps women reservists were photographed at Camp Lejeune, North Carolina, on October 16, 1943. They are, from left to right, Minnie Spotted Wolf, a Blackfoot, Celia Mix, Pottawatomie, and Viola Eastman, Chippewa.*

**LEFT** *The Pulitzer Prize-winning photograph of the raising of the American flag on Mount Suribachi during the battle of Iwo Jima by Associated Press photographer Joe Rosenthal. At the left of the picture is Ira Hayes, a Pima, along with Franklin Sousley, John Bradley, Harlon Block, Michael Strank, and Rene Gagnon. All but Bradley, a Navy corpsman, were U.S. Marines. Hayes, Bradley, and Gagnon survived the fight.*

It is easy to understand why, therefore, when the United States became embroiled in World War I, Native Americans enlisted in large numbers in the armed services. Young men, restricted from carrying out their traditional roles as hunters and warriors on the reservations, longed for the adventure and opportunity military service would bring. However, these young men's enthusiasm for enlistment was not always shared by their families and tribal elders. This was particularly true among those tribes that only a generation or two earlier had been battling the U.S. Army on their homelands.

Those who returned from World War I as veterans tended to be drawn to urban areas. With the military cutbacks made by the U.S. after World War I, few Indians remained in the service, but were forced instead to seek out what jobs they could find in the urban areas and port cities where

they were discharged. Others returned, somewhat discouraged, to the reservations after their brief experience of assimilation. There is no evidence to suggest that Native Americans were victims of racial prejudice in World War I any more than were African Americans. In the trenches of the European war, the man next to you was your best friend and protector no matter what his race.

During World War II, many more Native Americans answered the call of duty—a greater proportion, in fact, of their number than that of the general population. Tribal resistance to military service was no longer a major factor, as veterans of the previous war had, on the whole, benefited from their experience. Native Americans joined every branch of the U.S. Armed Services. Eskimos and Eyaks from Canada joined the Royal Navy, Army, and Air Corps alongside other Canadians. While some Native Americans were victims of racial discrimination in training camps—

**LEFT** *Private First Class Ira Hayes at age 19, ready to jump at the Marine Corps Paratroop School in 1943. He was one of the five Marines in the Iwo Jima flag-raising photograph. A reluctant celebrity after the war, he appeared as himself in the 1949 film Sands of Iwo Jima with John Wayne.*

## GENERAL CLARENCE L. TINKER

General Clarence L. Tinker, born in Oklahoma, was the son of George Edward Tinker, Sr. and Sarah Ann "Nan" Schwagerty. He was of Osage lineage and already a distinguished airman by the time the United States entered the Second World War. A two-star general, Tinker was commander of Hickam Air Force Base in Honolulu. After the success of the Doolittle Raid, Tinker planned an ambitious raid on Japanese-controlled Wake Island. He ordered four long-range bombers for the attack. After being outfitted and flown to Hawaii, the planes were readied for the mission. The first attempt to bomb the island was scrubbed due to bad weather and Tinker's plane was lost at sea. But the rest of the squadron returned to Wake Island in late June 1942 and carried out a highly successful raid, the first made at a range of more than 1,000 miles from base. The flyers had fulfilled Tinker's dream.

from stereotyping jokes to hazing—these actions and attitudes changed when the soldiers, sailors, airmen, and marines were sent overseas. As in World War I, American and Canadians of differing skin colors united in their fight against a common enemy.

At home, Native Americans got involved in the war effort in various ways. Women, or those too old to serve, worked in defense plants or provided support services to those who did. Women Native Americans also joined the Womens' Army Corps (W.A.C.S.) and Women Accepted for Vountary Emergency Service (W.A.V.E.S.) Others participated in civil defense teams. The extreme northern part of the continent was closer than any other part of North America to the air bases Germany was placing in Norway, Denmark, and Poland. The development of radar allowed the Allies to build an early-warning system with stations along the Arctic Circle. Many Canadian and Alaskan Eskimos worked in building and maintaining these stations. They would, during the Cold War a decade later, help construct the North American Aereospace Defense Command (N.O.R.A.D.) defense.

The heroics of Native Americans in World War II are too numerous to detail here, from Louie Adrian, a Spokane Indian who died fighting on Suribachi, to Walter Lawyer, a chief's descendant who served and died in Germany in 1945, and Tommy Prince, the most decorated Canadian of aboriginal descent. Native Americans have fought in Korea, Vietnam, and all the subsequent conflicts involving American troops. The stories mentioned here are dedicated to all Native Americans, living or dead, who served their two countries in the name of freedom.

**Document**
ITEM 11. Confidential documents that describe course work, including lessons for the use of the Navajo alphabet, its application to the transmission of secret wartime communications, and radio operator field duties in the training of Navajo code talkers in the U.S. Marine Corps, 1945.
(See pocket page 43.)

RIGHT TOP *Corporal George Miner, a member of the Winnebago tribe from Tomah, Wisconsin, poses for a U.S. Army Signal Corps photographer while on guard duty in 1919 at Niederähren, Germany at the end of World War I.*

RIGHT MIDDLE *U.S. Army Lieutenant Ernest Childers, a Creek, is congratulated by General Jacob L. Devers in 1944 after receiving the Congressional Medal of Honor in Italy for wiping out two machine-gun nests.*

RIGHT BOTTOM *Tobias William Frazier was a Choctaw from Oklahoma and served as a U.S. Army code talker in World War I.*

ABOVE *WWII bomber pilot Lieutenant Woody J. Cochran displays a captured Japanese flag in this photograph taken on New Guinea, April 1, 1943. A Cherokee from Oklahoma, Cochran earned the Silver Star, Purple Heart, Distinguished Flying Cross, and Air Medal.*

BELOW *A group of Native American U.S. Marines pose with their rifles during a World War II training exercise.*

# CODE TALKERS

"Code Talkers" was the nickname of those soldiers, members of the U.S. Navy and Marines, who used Native American languages to code transmissions and military dispatches, as a result denying vital information to the enemy. Although the largest and most famous group was the Navajo code talkers of World War II, Native American code talkers of various tribes had used their historic languages to baffle enemy interceptors during the two world wars. The code talkers of World War II acted as, or with, radio operators, confusing enemy listening posts and keeping the Allies' vital military dispatches secret.

# Urban Migration of Native Americans

The transition of Native Americans from the camps and communities of their homeland, to reservations, and then finally to the cities of America, was a long journey and prior to the 1930s, one made by very few Indians. Unlike African Americans who, after gaining their freedom as a result of the Union victory in the Civil War, flocked to the cities in large numbers in search of new opportunities and a better life, few American Indians saw cities in the same light. Indeed, the Dawes Act encouraged them to become farmers, tilling their own plots of land. The majority who did not take advantage of the program remained on the reservations, practicing traditional lifestyles, and seeing their affairs managed by the Bureau of Indian Affairs.

〜〜〜 ☥ 〜〜〜

There were, however, exceptions. Those Native Americans who attended public and private Indian boarding schools and learned new skills or continued into higher education were more liable to end up in cities than their fellow tribesmen. Those who excelled in adapting to the ways of the whites traveled to those places where their skills and knowledge were in demand—in industry, education, medicine, sports. Others gained opportunities and position by intermarriage. Most of these openings were typically available in or near the large cities.

Though the Mohawks and other Native American ironworkers succeeded in keeping the typical wages of Native American workers in the cities above the national average, some were not so fortunate. The lack of education forced many to accept low-paying jobs and they suffered from prejudice, particularly in the American northwest. Those who had a history of alcoholism or arrest could not land permanent employment. Often they were only employed in seasonal work or day labor. When they did get government jobs, they would find themselves in unfamiliar territory when those jobs ended. Many drifted back to the reservations.

Then in the 1950s, the U.S. government changed policy abruptly, and began to encourage more migration as part of the move towards termination of federal involvement in Indian affairs. Among the reasons for this about-face were the admission by the B.I.A. that the allotment policy was not working and the more insidious desire by

## IRONWORKERS

One group of Native Americans established a lasting reputation for their special skills. These were Mohawk men whose bravery and agility made them ideally suited for work on large building and civil construction projects. From a beginning as unskilled laborers on a bridge across the St. Lawrence River in Quebec, they spread out over the continent working on high steel bridge and building construction, including during the boom in steel-girder skyscrapers that sprang up in New York during the 1920s. The demand for their skills was so great that they frequently crossed the U.S.-Canadian border to practice their craft. After the tragedy of September 11, 2001, Native American ironworkers who had built the World Trade Center returned to advise officials on how it was constructed.

**ABOVE LEFT** *Kidd Smith, a Seneca woodcarver, at work in the Tonawanda Community House in western New York State in 1940. The Seneca and other New York tribes have maintained small reservation lands in the state.*

**LEFT** *(From left) Ironworkers John Tionekate Scott, Peter Atawakon Rice, Jim Ross, Adrian Bonnelly (non-native lawyer,) Joe Tehonate Albany, Paul Kanento Diabo, and Dominic Otseteken McComber were all involved in Diabo's successful 1927 challenge to U. S.-Canadian border crossing restrictions in U. S. District Court under the provisions of the 1794 Jay Treaty.*

**ABOVE** *Kahnawake Mohawk ironworkers Frank White, Julian Decaire, Angus Leclaire, Bill Meloche, Mack Montour, Joe Canadian, and friends pose for a picture on a high steel project.*

**BACKGROUND** *Native American ironworkers Angus Mitchell, Joseph J. Jocks, and Alex Fisher work on New York's United Nations Building in 1949.*

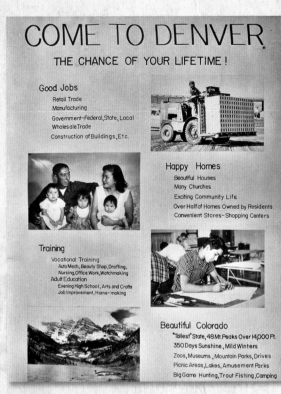

# COME TO DENVER
## THE CHANCE OF YOUR LIFETIME !

**Good Jobs**
Retail Trade
Manufacturing
Government-Federal, State, Local
Wholesale Trade
Construction of Buildings, Etc.

**Happy Homes**
Beautiful Houses
Many Churches
Exciting Community Life
Over Half of Homes Owned by Residents
Convenient Stores-Shopping Centers

**Training**
Vocational Training
Auto Mech., Beauty Shop, Drafting,
Nursing, Office Work, Watchmaking
Adult Education
Evening High School, Arts and Crafts
Job Improvement, Home-making

**Beautiful Colorado**
"Tallest" State, 48 Mt. Peaks Over 14,000 Ft.
350 Days Sunshine, Mild Winters
Zoos, Museums, Mountain Parks, Drives
Picnic Areas, Lakes, Amusement Parks
Big Game Hunting, Trout Fishing, Camping

**LEFT** *This poster from the 1940s encouraged Native Americans to leave the reservation behind and start a new life working in the burgeoning community of Denver. The campaign was part of a move by the Bureau of Indian Affairs to draw Native Americans off the reservations and into the workforce. It met with limited success.*

**RIGHT** *John Howe, a Washoe, poses in front of a furnace in the early 1900s when coal furnaces were stoked by hand. Industrialization and transportation began to replace agriculture and mining as the economic driving force in the American West toward the end of the nineteenth century.*

corporate and other interests to exploit the reservations for natural resources. Added to the pressure for jobs by returning veterans, the forced migration to the cities left many Native Americans unprepared for the change. Most ended up in the ghettos and Indian bars with little hope of self-improvement.

In the 1960s, the B.I.A. began to implement much-needed changes. They began from within, by bringing more Native Americans to work for the agency. Then, the director and the field officers made sure that federal training and education programs, such as the C.E.T.A. program of the 1970s, were applied to Native Americans in the cities. The B.I.A. also made sure that they monitored federal and state education and assistance programs to ensure they met the special needs of the Native American population. Native American opportunities and prosperity increased in urban areas and toward the end of the twentieth century roughly 45 percent of the Native American population in North America lived in or near cities.

**RIGHT** *Thomas Benyagka (right) holding the Hopi Prophecy with Bill Wapepah while Dennis Banks looks on at the Intertribal Friendship House, Oakland, California, in 1979. For many years, the intertribal centers were the only safe public places for Native Americans to gather in the cities to talk, exchange ideas, and observe the ceremonies of their heritage.*

**BOTTOM RIGHT** *Three teenagers in front of the Intertribal Friendship House in Oakland in 1972. The intertribal centers welcomed individuals and families of Native American heritage without judgment.*

**LEFT** *Joseph J. Jocks, a Kahnawake Mohawk, rivets a girder on the San Francisco Bay Bridge in the 1930s. The ironworkers traveled North America and even overseas to work on high steel projects.*

# Outstanding Native Americans

Singling out individuals from a group, such as those Native Americans featured here, is a risky proposition. The breadth of their individual achievements cannot be adequately described on these pages. Also, these individuals must be seen only as examples of many more Native Americans in recent years who have achieved public success and personal goals within or partially removed from their cultural heritage. All of those mentioned here have attained great public success, and bring a sense of pride and accomplishment to their people.

One of the early scholars of Native American descent to chronicle Indian culture from a historical perspective was Joseph Matthews, an Osage from Oklahoma. He studied at Oxford University, was a Rhodes Scholar, and served for eight years on the Osage tribal council. He wrote five books including a massive work on his tribe, *The Osages, Children of the Middle Waters*, which included research based on documents and interviews with long-time tribal members. His work was not limited to Native American studies. He also penned *Life and Death of An Oilman, the Career of E.W. Marland.*

Oklahoma-born Allie Reynolds was a Creek who showed a talent for pitching early in life. The right-handed pitcher, nicknamed "Superchief," came up through the Yankee organization and served at the major league level in baseball in the late 1940s and early 1950s. He earned 131 victories and was only recently passed by Andy Pettite for ninth place on the Yankee's all-time win list. He pitched in four World Series under Casey Stengal and threw two no-hitters, the only Yankee pitcher to do so, including one in the 1951 play-off run against Boston.

Maria Tallchief, an Osage, was prima ballerina for the prestigious New York City Ballet from 1947 to 1960. She received the "Woman of the Year Award" in 1953 from President Eisenhower and was named "Wa-Xthe-Thonba" or "Woman of Two Standards" by the Osage Tribal Council. She retired from the stage but continues to direct ballet for the Chicago Lyric Opera. Russell "Big Chief" Moore, a Pima Indian, was a fixture in the New York jazz scene of the 1950s and 60s. He played trombone behind Billie Holiday, Louis Armstrong, and many others.

Buffy Sainte-Marie was one of the most popular folk singers of the 1960s and one who changed contemporary perspectives about the appearance of an Indian maiden. In her numerous early concert tours,

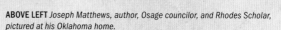

## JIM THORPE

Jacobus Franciscus "Jim" Thorpe was born in Indian Territory in 1887. His parents were both half-blood Indians but his mother was a descendant of Sauk-Fox Chief Black Hawk and he was raised in that tradition. Jim Thorpe was a medal winner in the 1912 Olympics in the pentathlon and decathlon, although his medals were taken away when it was discovered he had earlier played some minor league baseball. He later played major league baseball and played and coached for the Canton, Ohio football team, an original team in the National Football League (N.F.L.) He went on to play in 52 N.F.L. games. His Olympic medals were later reinstated and presented to his children in 1983.

**ABOVE LEFT** *Joseph Matthews, author, Osage councilor, and Rhodes Scholar, pictured at his Oklahoma home.*

**ABOVE** *A photograph of Maria Tallchief when she was at the height of her performance career with the New York City Ballet. Her husband, George Balanchine, served for many years as the company's principal choreographer.*

**LEFT** *Buffy Saint Marie performs at a National Aeronautics and Space Administration (NASA) event. Another popular Native American Grammy winner is Robbie Robertson of The Band.*

she sang and played guitar in jeans, boots, and cotton shirts. Only later did she sometimes appear in costume attributed to her roots as a Canadian Cree. Her popularity as a singer-songwriter gained world appeal and her song "Until It's Time for You to Go" was recorded by Elvis, Cher, and Barbra Streisand. She produced 18 albums including compilations and earned several Grammys and an Oscar. In recent years she has been involved in educational interests as well—she has a doctoral degree in education—and has worked with the television program Sesame Street, tribal groups, and her own youth foundation.

Another Grammy winner is Mary Youngblood. Trained as a classical flutist, she earned the award for "Beneath the Raven Moon," one of several disks she has produced with the six-hole Native flute. She continues to work as a performer, composer, and educator. Likewise, Native American performer Wayne Newton has touched the lives of millions for decades.

Waneek Horn-Miller was assistant captain of the Canadian water polo team at the 2000 Olympics and remains active in Canadian athletics today. She has a deep appreciation for the accomplishments of Native American Olympians who came before her: "Alwyn Morris, 1984 Olympic kayak gold medalist, was the first Canadian aboriginal gold medal winner and is a Mohawk from my community. Sharon and Shirley Firth, Dene Native Americans from the Northwest Territories, are three-time Olympians in cross-country skiing. Billy Mills, 1964 ten-kilometer runner, won the only gold medal in track and field that year for the U.S. He's a Sioux from Pine Ridge, South Dakota."

The only Native American to serve in the United States Senate is Ben Nighthorse Campbell. He was born in Oklahoma but enlisted early in the services and later relocated to Colorado. An injury forced an end to his career in international competitive judo and he became interested in politics. He served in the Colorado General Assembly, the U.S. House of Representatives and two terms as one of Colorado's U.S. Senators, retiring in 2005.

## WILL ROGERS

William Penn Adair "Will" Rogers was born in 1879 on Dog Iron Ranch in Indian Territory to parents of Cherokee heritage. Always in love with cowboy culture, he developed a trick roping act and performed in Florenz Ziegfeld's Follies in New York, adding a comic patter that soon made him one of the show's most popular performers. He obtained roles in silent films, and then went to Hollywood, becoming one of the most popular movie stars, and, at the height of the Great Depression, an influential performer and columnist in radio and print. An avid early supporter of aviation, he died in a plane crash at Point Barrow, Alaska, on 15 August 1935, and was much mourned by a shocked nation.

DEDICATION
*Will Rogers*
FIELD
OKLAHOMA CITY
JUNE 28, 1941

**LEFT** *Waneek Horn-Miller, who graduated from Carlton University in 1999 with a political science degree, has won medals in numerous Canadian amateur competitions in addition to representing her country at the 2000 Sydney Olympics.*

ALLIE REYNOLDS
*pitcher* NEW YORK YANKEES

**ABOVE** *Two-term United States Senator from Colorado Ben Nighthorse Campbell.*

**LEFT** *Amazing pitcher Allie Reynolds pictured in New York Yankee pinstripes on his 1954 trading card.*

**FAR LEFT** *Brian Trottier, born in Saskatchewan to a Cree/Chippewa father, was a former National Hockey League Rookie of the Year. He holds many personal scoring records and helped the New York Islanders to win four Stanley Cups in 1980–84.*

# Native American Art and Literature

At the beginning of the twentieth century, the emergence of Indian schools—those on the reservations and the longer-established boarding schools—gave rise to an increased number of Native Americans literate in the English language and versed in a broad array of cultures. As a result, Native American authors have produced a prolific body of literature over the past century. Whether in fiction, social commentary, or scholarly or spiritual works, they have competed on an equal basis with authors of other races. Likewise, a New Deal era emphasis on art and crafts sparked a renaissance in traditional methods and a transition to broader artistic expression among Indian artists.

Native Americans are often portrayed as serious in dramatic productions, but they like to laugh. Often, Native American authors and artists cannot help but poke fun or write serious criticism about how the race is perceived by others. The general unfamiliarity with detailed history, combined with the stereotyping of Native Americans in popular media has given a skewed view of their culture. The film *Smoke Signals* (1998) achieved great acclaim for its exploration of this theme. Many other Indian artists and writers look at how they are perceived and how they see themselves. This sort of biting commentary is evident in David Bradley's painting, *American Indian Gothic* (1983.) Bradley is of Chippewa and Lakota descent.

Though he often uses humor in his public expressions on the condition of Native Americans, Adam Fortunate Eagle takes his art seriously. After learning the art of pipe-making, he studied art techniques at Haskell Institute under muralist Franklin Gritts, and sculptor and muralist Allen Houser. His sculptures are legendary. But sometimes his sense of humor works its way into his art, as in his installation art statement *a tire lodge on a Paiute-Shoshone reservation*. Another Native American artist who possesses the talent to capture a sense of history is Indian Joe Morris. Morris was a longshoreman in San Francisco during the occupation of Alcatraz Island by Native Americans. He sought support for the occupiers from his union and received unanimous

ABOVE *A collage by Arthur Amiotte. In this work the artist combines his own hand-drawn Native American caricatures with scenes appearing in a French journal.*

approval. His unusual paintings use the materials around which he worked while helping to load supply boats for the occupiers.

Native American artists work in all media. A number of them work with some degree of traditional Indian craft forms. Jenny Ann "Chapoose" Taylor created an American flag entirely from beads in 2002. It is on display at the Smithsonian National Museum of the American Indian on the National Mall in Washington. The museum also features the work of Melissa Cody, an award-wining young Navajo weaver.

Arthur Amiotte is a Lakota artist who was born on the Pine Ridge Reservation and is a descendant of Chief Standing Bear. A studied artist and teacher, he now specializes in collages, using family and public images in combination with his drawings and written narrative. He often includes ledger-book drawings, a traditional form of Lakota art of the nineteenth century, and uses the automobile as a frequent metaphor for his themes of contrasting conditions.

Native American artists often mix traditional and modern themes in works of pottery, basketry, and hide and feather creations. The same is true of writers, both of poetry and prose, who celebrate Native American culture using themes and characters from the past and present. The immense spiritualism of the culture is evident in many works. America Meredith, an upcoming artist, sees her works negotiating the interactions

## R.C. GORMAN

R.C. Gorman is a Navajo artist who has been compared to Picasso for his stylized drawings and prints. His early works in the 1980s and '90s were renditions of Navajo blankets, but he quickly turned his attention to drawing Indian female nudes, a major portion of his body of work. In later years, after having gained acclaim for his drawings, he studied under master printer José Sanchez in Mexico City and added a series of prints, known as the Indian "madonnas," to his expanding collection of internationally acclaimed works. He died in 2005 while still a very prolific artist.

TOP (BACKGROUND)
*Jenny Ann "Chapoose" Taylor, a member of the Uintah tribe of Utah, created this American flag using 130,910 glass beads sewn onto leather with nylon thread. The 23 x 33 inch (58 x 85 cm) work displays the names of tribes of the United States in the stripes and state abbreviations as the stars.*

ABOVE *The Seeing, a public art sculpture by Johnny Bear Contreras for the Poway, California City Hall, is the result of the artist's interpretation of the transition from the physical world to the spiritual realm.*

ABOVE FAR LEFT
*American Indian Gothic, a lithograph on paper by David Bradley is of course a parody of the famous Grant Wood painting, American Gothic. Realizing that "Indians are, by definition, political beings," Bradley decided to make a satiric comment on corruption of Indian values in the art world with the 1983 work.*

between humans, animals, plants, and spirits. She also likes to explore the space between Native and non-native, being of Cherokee, Swedish, and Celtic descent. "Instead of documenting cross-cultural conflicts, I am interested in portraying those Native and European Americans who could find common ground," she says. Her award-winning work also includes Cherokee symbolism, such as characters from the unique Cherokee alphabet.

Award-winning young sculptor Johnny Bear Contreras, a member of California's Kumeyaay tribe, finds satisfaction in creating public art. He has created stirring works for the cities of Poway and Santa Fe Springs, California, and the Cathedral of Our Lady of the Angels in Los Angeles. His flowing, dynamic style is a reflection of his life transitions, from his youth on the San Pasqual Reservation, via the development of his talent through a combination of formal training and working in the building trades to support his family, and finally to his status as a sought-after sculptor. He reflects on the philosophy that drives his vision: "Often times man can be moving like liquid, or sedentary like stone. He may be slumped on the steps that society has placed before him or he might have created the steps on which he will fall. The steps might also be for advancement."

Indian artists now enjoy the acceptance of a worldwide audience. The works of painters, sculptors, photographers, and muralists are displayed in public buildings, museums, and galleries throughout the world. An annual Native American film and video festival brings together animation, documentary, dramatic, and short subject creations produced by Indian masters of the audio-visual arts. When many of these new works are introduced to the public, whether fine artworks, craft renditions, written word, performances, or filmed entertainment, the Native American creators are involved in a dual function—celebrating the creative interpretation of their heritage while also cementing the contribution of Native Americans to the worlds of contemporary art and literature.

> *"I long for the day when Native American is a description of the literary work and not the deciding definition."*
> **Sherman Alexie 2007**

## SHERMAN ALEXIE

Sherman J. Alexie, Jr. was born in 1966 on a reservation in Wellpinit, Washington, 50 miles (80 km) from Spokane, and is a Spokane/Coeur d'Alene Indian. Seizures and other side effects of hydrocephaly as an infant kept him something of a loner; but he avidly pursued knowledge and attended Gonzaga University and Washington State, where he received his degree and encouragement in poetry writing. He won several awards for his poetry, wrote short stories for *The Atlantic Monthly* and published a novel. A film based on his work, *Smoke Signals*, won several awards at the 1998 Sundance Film Festival and was commercially released. Today, he is much sought after as a critic, humorist, and television personality in the Seattle area.

# Moving Forward, Without Forgetting the Past

Native Americans who were educated and grew up in the period of assimilation following World War II, saw the large-scale activism that swept the United States and Canada in the 1960s and 70s (as a result of continuing racial strife and opposition to the war in Vietnam) as an opportunity to demonstrate against government policies and racial stereotyping.

Following the occupation of "the rock", a group of activists organized by the American Indian Movement (A.I.M.) caravanned to Washington, D.C. to have a list of grievances addressed. Largely ignored, they embarked on a series of peaceful occupations across the nation. But by then, a policy of allowing the tribes self-determination without abandonment by the federal government was beginning to take shape.

Native Americans began to manage their own affairs at tribal level, while taking advantage of the federal protection and aid offered to them as a long-suffering, disenfranchised people. The Indians quickly learned how to use statutes and politics to achieve the desired ends. The Pequot tribe of Connecticut was the first to succeed with a large-scale gaming operation on reservation land, building the grand Foxwoods Resort-Casino in 1992.

While Indian casinos use limited reservation land effectively and provide their tribes with income for municipal and social services, many Native Americans consider them a vice, inconsistent with tribal and cultural values. But there is no denying that as the economic muscle behind the right of self-determination, the casinos have had the largest impact of any development on Native American Culture entering the new millennium.

## ADAM FORTUNATE EAGLE—ACTIVIST

Adam Fortunate Eagle has been a major force in shaping Native American progress for over 40 years. Born in Minnesota to a Swedish father and Chippewa mother, he attended Pipestone Indian Training School. He started a small business in San Leandro, California, but became concerned about the trauma experienced by Indians who were driven into cities. He was instrumental in starting intertribal support organizations in the San Francisco Bay area. He became a prominent leader statewide and was invited to Washington to give the Native American perspective as the Lyndon Johnson administration launched the "War on Poverty" in 1964. He was also involved in the occupation of the vacant Alcatraz Federal Penitentiary in 1969.

## THE OCCUPATION OF ALCATRAZ

In November 1969, after years of serious attempts to take over the former federal penitentiary for Indian use failed, a group of Native Americans seized Alcatraz Island in San Francisco harbor and occupied it for 19 months. They offered to "buy" the island for $24 in order to establish a Native American culture and education center there. The demonstrators held press conferences, attracting international and celebrity support. Over time, the number of demonstrators on "the Rock" diminished, and the last Indians were removed by U.S. Marshals on June 11, 1971. Although the occupation did not appear to be a clear-cut victory for Native Americans, it soon became evident that public awareness of their demands had been raised.

**FAR LEFT** *The San Pasqual Fire Department maintains fire prevention and control programs in addition to being ready to deal with any emergency on the reservation in the arid hills of northeast San Diego County.*

**BELOW** *Indian occupiers of Alcatraz waiting to greet new arrivals to the island. The "Indians of All Tribes," as the occupiers referred to themselves, came from many parts of the U.S. and Canada, and most were students. They held the island from November 10, 1969 until U.S. Marshals removed the last 15 occupiers on June 11, 1971.*

**LEFT** *The main entrance to the Foxwoods Resort-Casino. The rural Connecticut location of the casino has not been a hindrance to its popularity.*

**LEFT** *A Havasupai rodeo staged in northwestern Arizona in 1947. A popular and lasting tradition of Native American cultures of the west is the rodeo.*

## PRESERVING NATIVE AMERICAN HERITAGE

Native American culture is experiencing a period of unprecedented growth. The recent establishment of the Smithsonian National Museum of the American Indian marks a new visibility to the study and exhibition of the culture. Throughout the United States and Canada, many other new museums, cultural centers, and historic sites are being established. Nearly all major universities and colleges have programs of Native American studies. Seminars and other opportunities to bring Native Americans and non-natives together for mutual understanding are on the rise. Because this growth is dynamic, an archive of new information will continue beyond this work.

But even though Native Americans—whether living on reservations among their own people or in houses and apartments in cities and suburbs—embrace many aspects of modern society, it doesn't mean they drift away from their culture and past. Pow-wows, harvest festivals and educational and cultural exchanges are popular forms of interchange and enjoyment for many Native Americans. And, when welcomed in, they have a positive impact on people of other cultures as well. Museums and cultural centers have been created from tribal resources in an effort to involve the public in understanding the complex culture and history of the tribe and of Native Americans as a people. Many national museums and institutions foster study and involvement in the cultures of the various tribes and Native Americans in general, as an important segment of the population, whose people are to be commended for their patience, admired for their courage, and embraced for their unique contribution to the world, now and in times past and future.

## POW-WOWS

Pow-wows, both tribal and intertribal, give families, tribal members, and even those distantly connected, the opportunity to meet or reunite and exchange news and ideas first hand. In most cases dance and craft demonstrations, food, and object displays are open to all. Museum founder Carl Bornfriend (Lenape,) of the Frisco Native American Museum in Hatteras, North Carolina, is very proud of the long-running annual pow-wow there. "Our Pow-wow, 'Journey Home,' is the result of one of humankind's longest-running needs and traditions. We are most gratified to celebrate on ancient ancestral ground where ALL are welcome in peace, love, and appreciation."

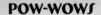

**ABOVE** *This beaded horse-head cover, sewn onto rawhide, was used by a Lakota chief to lead the 1904 Fourth of July parade at Pine Ridge Agency, South Dakota. The patriotic event, held less than 14 years after the Ghost Dance uprising and massacre at the agency, was a testament to the ability of the people to overcome terrible tragedy and look to the future.*

# Index

## A

Abnaki tribe 25
Acorn People 26-27
Adena People 8-9
Adobe Walls, Battle of 39
Adobe Walls, Texas 44
African Americans 34
agriculture 8, 13, 16, 21, 26, 33, 36, 45, 55
Alabama 31, 34
Alaska 29-31, 48
Alcatraz Island, occupation of 59, 60, 60
Aleut language 29, 29
Aleutian Islands 28, 46, 46
Aleuts 28-29, 46
Algonquian languages 10, 16, 28
Allegheny River 25
Alta California 26-27
American Indian Movement 60
Anasazi tribe 12-13, 18, 18
Apache Pass, Arizona 39
Apache Pass, Battle of 44
Apache tribes 13, 50
Apalachee tribe 22
Appalachians 20
Appomattox, Confederate surrender at 38
Arapaho tribe 45
Archaic Stage 8-9
Arctic 7, 28-29, 46
Arikara tribe 32-33
Arizona 45, 51
Army, U. S. Native Americans in the 52
Assiniboin tribe 35
Athapaskan languages 13, 16, 28
Attu, Alaska 46, 46
Aztec Ruins, New Mexico 12

## B

Bad Axe River, Battle of 31
Bannock tribe 36
basket weaving 8, 37
Bear Creek, Idaho, massacre at 39
Benyagka, Thomas 55
Beringia 6-7
Big Foot 43, 43
Big Mound, Battle of 38
Billy Bowlegs (Alligator Chief) 22
Biloxi tribe 40
Birch Coulee, Battle of 38
bison 32-34, 33, 34, 41
Black Beaver 11
Black Hawk 31, 56
Black Hills 42-43
Black Kettle 39, 39, 43
Blackfeet 33, 33, 35, 46, 50, 50, 52
Blackfoot see Blackfeet tribe
Bonita Pueblo, New Mexico 14
Bornfriend, Carl 62
Bounty, for proof of kill or capture of Native Americans 27
bows and arrows 15, 15
Bozeman Trail 42, 42, 43
Bradenton, Florida 22
Brown, Governor Joseph 39
Buck Watie (Elias Boudinot) 20, 20
buffalo see bison
Buffalo Bill Cody 52
Bureau of Indian Affairs 35, 39, 48, 50-51, 54-55, 60
burial sites 9, 9, 35

## C

Cahokia, Illinois 9
calendars 32
caliche buildings 13, 13
California 36-37
Calusa tribe 22
Cameahwait 33
Canada 10, 31-3, 49, 50-51
Canassatego 24
cannibalism 22
Cannonball River 39
canoes 10, 16
Carlisle Indian Industrial School 48, 49, 50
Carmel, Mission 26
Casa Grande 13, 13
casinos 60
Catawba nation 20, 21,

35, 34
Cauhnawaga tribe 30
Cayuga nation 10, 11
ceremonies 19, 19, 20, 37, 40, 40, 41, 41
Chawasiu tribe 40
Chelly, Canyon de 12, 12
Cherokee language 21, 21
Cherokee Nation 20, 21, 23, 25, 30, 31, 34, 35, 38, 39, 40, 41, 51, 53
Cheyenne River 35
Cheyenne River Agency 43
Cheyenne tribes 31, 32, 39, 38, 40, 42, 43, 44
Chickasaw nation 20, 21, 30, 31, 35, 39
Chinook tribe 16, 17
Chippewa tribe 49, 51, 55
Chiricahua Apache tribe 39, 44, 45, 46
Chitimacha tribe 40
Choctaw nation 20, 21, 23, 30, 31, 34, 35, 39, 48
Chokonens 44
Chumash tribe 24, 25
Chustenahlah, Battle of 37
Cibola, Seven Cities of see Seven Cities of Cibola
citizenship, U. S. for Native Americans 49
Citrus County, Florida 23
Civil War, American 12, 19, 38-39
Civilian Conservation Corps, Indian Division 50, 51
Clayquot tribe 29
Clearwater River 33
Coast Salish tribe 17
Cochise 39, 44, 44, 45
Code talkers 53
Colonies, European 15, 22
colonists, attacks on 23
Colorado 39, 42
Columbia River 16, 17, 32, 33
Columbus, Christopher 22
Comanche nation 13, 39, 40, 41, 44, 45
Commissioner of Indian Affairs 38
Confederates 21
Connecticut 10, 14, 
Conquistadors 22
Continental Army 30
Continental Congress 20
Contreras, Johnny Bear 59
Copper Eskimos 46
Coronado, Francisco Vásquez de 12, 12, 13, 18
crafts 23, 26, 37, 48, 48, 51
Crazy Horse 42, 43
Creek Indian War 31
Creek tribe 20, 21, 22, 23, 25, 31, 34, 33, 37, 51, 54
Cross County, Arkansas 9
Crow tribe 32, 42
Cupertino Mission Indians 27
Custer, Gen. George Armstrong 42-43

## D

Dakota language 35
Dakota Territory 38
Dakota tribe (Santee Sioux) 32, 33, 38, 39, 42
Dawes Act 48, 49, 49, 50
Dawes, Sen. Henry 48
Dead Buffalo Lake, Battle of 39
Declaration of Allegiance 49
Deganawidah 10
Delaware Colony 14
Delaware tribe (Lenape) 10, 11, 15
Dene tribe 57
Denver, Colorado 39, 55
disease 11, 14, 22, 40
hogans 13, 19, 19
Do-Gïägyä-Gúát 45

## E

East St. Louis, Illinois 9
Erik the Red 28
El Dorado 12, 13, 22
El Paso, Texas 19

Emancipation Proclamation of California Tribes 27, 27
Erie, Lake 30
Eskimos 7, 8, 28, 28, 29, 46, 52, 53
Espiritu Santo 20
Etowah River 21
Eyak tribe 28, 46, 50

## F

Fallen Timbers, Battle of 30
First World War 52
fishing 17, 23, 29, 36, 36, 46, 47
Five Civilized Tribes 35, 38, 39, 41, 48
Flagstaff, Arizona 19
Florida 7, 22, 31, 34
Folsom, New Mexico 6, 7
Forest Service, U. S. 51
Fort Abraham Lincoln, North Dakota 43
Fort Bowie, Arizona 39, 44, 45
Fort Caroline, Florida 22-23, 23
Fort Duquesne, Pennsylvania 24, 25
Fort Laramie, Second Treaty of 42, 42
Fort Laramie, Wyoming 34, 35, 42
Fort McKenzie, Montana 33, 33
Fort Marion, Florida 44, 45, 49
Fort Moultrie, South Carolina 34
Fort Necessity, Pennsylvania 25
Fort Niagara, New York 25
Fort Oswego, New York 25
Fort Pitt, Pennsylvania 25
Fort Rice, North Dakota 39
Fort Ridgely, Minnesota 38
Fort Ridgely, Battle of 38
Fort San Mateo, Florida 23
Fort Sill, Oklahoma 42, 43
Fort Snelling, Minnesota 38
Fort Vancouver, Washington 16
Fort Wayne, Treaty of 31
Fort William McHenry, New York 25
Four Corners 12, 18
Fox tribe 11, 30, 30, 31
Foxwoods Casino Resort 61, 61
Franciscans see also missionaries 27
Franklin, Benjamin 24
Fredericksburg Peace Council 41, 41
Fredericksburg, Texas 41
Frémont, John C. 36
French and Indian War 24

## G

Georgia 21, 23, 31, 34, 35
Geronimo 44, 45, 45
Ghost Dance movement 40, 41
Gila Cliff Dwelliings 13, 13
gold 34, 36, 37, 42, 43, 45
Gorman, R. C. 58

Grant, Ulysses S. 38, 42
Great Lakes 30
Greenland 28, 47
Greenville, Treaty of 30
Guale tribe 22

## H

Haida tribe 16
Havasupai tribe 13, 51
Hawikuh Pueblo, New Mexico 19
Hiawatha 10, 10
Hidatsa tribe 33
Highway to the Sun 50, 50
Hispaniola 22
hogans 13, 19, 19
Hohokam tribe 13, 26
Holms, Thomas Campanius 15
Homestead Act 48
Honey Springs, Battle of 39
Hopewell People 9, 10
Hopewell, Treaty of 30
Hopi see Mogollón tribe

Hopi Prophecy 55
Horn-Miller, Waneek 57, 57
horses 7, 12, 12, 18, 32
Horseshoe Bend, Battle of 21, 23, 31, 34
houses, Native American 10, 11, 13, 17, 18, 18, 19, 19, 20, 21, 21, 26, 28, 28, 29, 33, 34, 49
Hudson River 15
Hudson's Bay Company 16, 29
Hunkpapa tribe 42, 49
Hupa tribe 36, 36, 37
Huron tribe 10, 14, 15

## I

Ice Age 6
Idaho 36, 41
igloos 28, 28
Illinois 34
Illinois militia 31
Independence, War of American 21, 30
Indian Affairs, Bureau of 34
Indian Agents 35, 34
Indian Department 35
Indian Home Guard 39
Indian Relocation Act 35
Indian Removal Act 31, 39
Indian Territories, removal to 20, 22, 31, 34, 35, 35, 38, 44, 49
Indian Territory 35, 39
Indian Territory, final disappearance of 48
Indiana/Indiana Territory 31, 34
integration 49
Inuits 46
Inupiats 47
Iowa 33
Iroquoian languages 10, 11
Iroquois Confederacy 11,15, 24
Iroquois People 14, 20, 25
Irrigation 13, 13
Iwo Jima, Battle of 52, 52

## J

Jackson, Andrew 21, 23, 31, 34, 35
Jamestown Settlement 15
Jay Treaty 54
Jefferson, Thomas 31, 32, 33, 36
jewelry 9, 11, 16, 17, 37
Jocks, Joseph 55
Johnson, Gen. William 24
Johnson, Lyndon B. 55

## K

Kachinas 19, 19
Kahnawake 55
Kaiser, H. G. 47
Kansas 39, 42, 44
kayaks 29, 29, 47, 47
Kentucky 34
Kentucky militia 30, 30
Keokuk 31
Killdeer Mountain, Battle of 39
King George's War 25
Kiowa Apache tribe 40, 44
Kiowa tribe 13, 32, 39, 40, 44, 45
kiva 19
Klamath tribe 51
Knik, Alaska 47
koshares 19, 19
Kotsina River 46
Kumeyaay band 26, 59
Kwakiutl tribe 16

## L

Labrador 28
Lake George, Battle of 24, 24
Lake Manix, California 6
Lakota tribe (Teton Sioux) 32, 33, 38, 40, 42, 42, 43, 32
Lame Deer 43
land grants to Native Americans 27
land sales to Europeans 11, 11, 14, 14
League of Iroquois Nations see Iroquois Confederacy
Lewis and Clark Expedition 31, 32, 32, 33
Lincoln, Abraham 38, 39, 39
liquor 15, 41, 46
Little Arkansas, Treaty

of 44
Little Bighorn, Battle of 42, 43, 43
Little Crow 38, 38
Little Missouri River 39
Littlefeather, Sacheem 61, 61
Lituya Bay, Alaska 16, 29
Llano River 41
Logstown, Ohio 24
London, visit by Iroquois chiefs 10
Long Island, New York 35
Louis XV, King 24
Louisiana 32, 34
Louisiana Purchase 30
Lower Sioux Agency 38
Luiseños 26

## M

Major Ridge 21, 21
Makah tribe 16
Malden, Ontario 30
Malibu, California 26, 27
mammoths 6, 7
Mandan tribe 32, 33, 33, 40
Mangas, Colorado 39, 44,
Manhattan 11
Manifest Destiny 40
Mankato, Minnesota 38, 39
Marshall, John 31, 34, 37
Mashantucket Pequot Museum, 60
Mashantucket Pequot tribe 59
masks 8
Massachuset tribe 8
Massachusetts Bay Colony 12
Massasoit 14
Mato-Tope 32
Matthews, Joseph 56, 56
Maximilian, Prince 31, 33, 34
McComber, Dominic Otsetokan 54
McElmo Canyon, Colorado 33
Medicine Lodge, Treaty of 43, 44
Menéndez de Avilés, Pedro 23
Menominee tribe 51
Mesa Verde National Park, Colorado 18, 18
mesas 18, 18
Meso Indians 8
Meusebach Treaty 41, 41
Meusebach, John O. 41
Mexican army 45
Mexico, government of 27
Miami tribe 11, 30
Michigan/Michigan Territory 31, 34
Micmac tribe 10
migration from Asia 6
Minnesota 34, 38, 51
Minnesota River 38
Mission Indians 26, 37
missionaries 15, 19, 20, 26, 27, 29, 35
missionaries, killing of 19
Missions 26, 26, 27
Mississippi Territory 30
Mississippian Culture 9
Missouri 39
Missouri River 32, 35
Missouri tribe 33, 34
Mogollón tribe (Hopi) 18, 18, 19, 26,
Mohave tribe 13
Mohawk tribe (Maqua) 10, 11, 25, 54, 55
Mojave Desert, California 6, 7
Mono tribe 36, 37
Monongahela River 24, 24, 25
Montana/Montana Territory 42, 43, 50, 51
Montcalm, Marquis de (Louis Jordan) 25, 25
Monterey, California 37
Mount Hood, Oregon 17
Mount Rainier, Washington 17
Mungoab 11
Munsee Delaware tribe 11

## N

Naches see Naiche
Naiche 44
Nakota tribe 38, 42
Nanticoke tribe 10
Nantucket tribe 34
Narraganset 10, 14
Natchez tribe 23, 23, 40

National Indian Memorial, New York 49
Navajo alphabet 53
Navajo code 53
Navajo nation 12, 13, 18, 19, 48
Nea-Math-La 22
Nebraska 33, 48
Netsvetov, Fr. Iakov 29, 29
Nevada 37
New Deal, The 50-51
New Echota, Georgia 34
New England 11, 11
New France 15, 24, 25
New Mexico 12, 39, 44, 45
New Netherlands 11, 11
New Orleans, Battle of 23
New Orleans, Louisiana 32
New Spain 12
New Sweden 15, 15
New Ulm 38
New York 11
Nez Percé 33
No Two Horns, Joseph 49
Noatak, Alaska 47
Nootka tribe (Nuu-Chah-Nulth) 16, 17, 29
Nordwall, Adam Fortunate Eagle 60, 60, 61, 61
Norsemen 28
North Carolina 15, 51
North Dakota 38, 39, 42, 51
Northwest Territory 30, 31
Nova Scotia 15, 24
Nunivak Island, Alaska 29
Nuu-Chah-Nulth see Nootka tribe

## O

Oglala Sioux see Lakota tribe
Ohio 30, 31, 34
Ohio Valley 24, 25
Ojibwa tribe 11
Oklahoma 48
Old Copper People 9
Old Fort Wayne, Battle of 39
Old Gabriel 26
Old Harbor, Alaska 29
Olympics, Stockholm 48
Oñate, Juan de 13, 19
Oneida nation 10, 11, 24, 30
Onondaga nation 10, 11
Opothleyahola 39
Oregon/Oregon Territory 5, 41, 51
Oregon Trail 34, 42
Osage tribe 32, 52, 56
Osceola 34, 34, 35
Oto(e) tribe 33, 34
Ottawa tribe 11, 30

## P

Paiute tribe 36, 41
Paleo-Indians 6
Palo Duro Canyon, Texas 44
Pamunkey tribe 15, 34
Pan'kov, Ivan 29
Papagos tribe 11
Patascus 14
paternalism, U. S. government's policy of 31
Pawnee nation 33
Pea Ridge, Battle of 38, 38
peace medals 31, 34
Pennsylvania 11, 15
Pennsylvania Gazette 24
Penobscot tribe 10
Pensacola, Florida 23
Pequot tribe 10, 14
Perry, Oliver Hazard 30
petroglyphs 8
Peyote Cult 44
Piapot band 56
pictographs 6, 8, 27, 27, 49
Piegan tribe 33, 33
Pima tribe 13, 52, 56
Piman languages 13
Pine Ridge Reservation 60
pipes 11, 33
Pisehedwin 50, 50
Pittsburgh, Pennsylvania 24, 25
Plains Indians 32, 40
Plains of Abraham 25
Pleistocene epoch 6
Plymouth Colony 14
Pocahontas 14, 14, 15
Point Barrow, Alaska 47
Pomeioc, North Carolina 21, 21
Pomo tribe 6, 37

Ponca tribe 34
Ponce de Léon, Juan 22
Pontchartrain, Lake 34
Pop Warner 50, 50
Pope, Maj. Gen. John 38, 39
Port of France, Alaska 29, 29
Portolá, Don Gaspár de 27
Potawatomie tribe 31, 48, 50, 50, 52
pow-wows 62
Powder Face 31
Powder River 42, 43
Powhatan Confederacy 14, 15
Powhatan tribe 10
Pratt, Richard Henry 49
Presidio, San Diego 26
Prudhoe Bay, Alaska 47
Pueblo Indians 13-15

## Q

Quahada Comanches 44
Quanah Parker 44, 44
Quapaw tribe 32
Quary, Abraham 34
Quebec 14, 15
Quebec, Battle and Siege of 25, 25
Quinault tribe 16, 17

## R

Red Cloud 42, 43, 43
Red Paint People 9, 10
Red Sticks 21, 23, 34
religion see spirituality; Christianity American
Rocky Mountains 32, 33, 36
Roosevelt, Franklin D. 50, 51
Rosebud, Battle of the 43

## S

Sac tribe see Sauk tribe
Sacajawea 33, 33
Sacramento, California 37
Sainte-Marie, Buffy 56, 56
Saladin Watie 40, 41
Salish tribe 16
Salt River 13
San Carlos Borromeo de Carmelo,Mission 26
San Diego de Alcalá, Mission 26, 26, 27
San Francisco Solano Mission 27
San Gabriel, Mission 26
San Luis Obispo, Mission 26
Sand Creek, Colorado, massacre at 39, 39
Santa Barbara, California 26
Santa Fe, New Mexico 19
Santa Fe Trail 39, 42, 44
Santee Sioux see Dakota tribe
Saratoga, Battle of 30
Sauk tribe (Sac) 31,31,32, 56
Scaraouady 4, 24
seal hunting 29, 47, 47
Seattle, Battle of 41,41

Second World War 51, 52
secularization, 26, 27
Seminole nation 21, 22, 22, 23, 23, 31, 34, 35, 39, 51
Seminole Wars 31, 34, 35
Seneca Reservation 48
Seneca nation 10, 11, 38, 54
Sequoyah (George Geist) 21, 21
Seven Cities of Cibola 12, 18, 19
Seven Years' War 25
Shackamaxon 15, 15
Shawnee tribe 30, 31
Shenandoah 43
Shinnecock tribe 35, 35
Shoshone tribe 32, 33
Sierra Nevada 36
Siouan languages 11
Sioux uprising 39
sipapu 18, 18, 19
Sitting Bull 42, 42
Sitting Bull the Minor (or Good) 42
Skagit tribe 17
Sloan Canyon, Nevada 27
South Carolina 22
South Dakota 35, 4 2, 51